Turning points –
a lifetime in transport

by

J. W. Womar
M.Inst.T., MIRTE (rtd)

Edited by Alan Townsin

Venture *publications*

ISBN 1 898432 58 9

DEDICATION

To Dad and Mum

Produced for the Publishers
Venture Publications, Glossop, Derbyshire,
by Mopok Graphics, Glossop SK13 8EH
using computerised origination

CONTENTS

INTRODUCTION

I have known Walter Womar for about 28 years, meeting first when he was General Manager of Midland Red and beginning to grapple with the succession of problems he met during his spell there, some a foretaste of those that would hit much of the industry as a whole a little later. I was then Editor of *'Bus & Coach'* magazine and thus attempting to ensure that I had a balanced picture of the whole industry. Midland Red held a special place as the biggest bus company in the country, second only to London Transport in fleet size, so I made several visits to Midland House during the late 'sixties and early 'seventies.

The Womar name already had quite a ring within the bus industry, beginning with the previous J. W. Womar, his father, one of that band of almost legendary figures who built up motor bus operation from its early uncertainties into a thoroughly professional business, having begun his career with one of the British Electric Traction tramway systems in 1908. I never met J. W. Womar senior, but saw enough of the North Western Road Car Co Ltd under his management when my parents moved within its area in 1941 to know that high standards were upheld, even in wartime. One never saw a scruffy North Western bus and the staff always looked the part too. Services may have been sparse under wartime fuel restrictions but I cannot recall a bus failing to turn up or be on time, and Walter's recollections of his father were thus of special interest.

There is a tendency for later generations, not least of politicians of almost any hue, to rather dismiss the methods of the past. Yet, looking back to those days when the measures in the 1930 Road Traffic Act had given operators a degree of security, the avoidance of direct competition on any given route did not, as might have been thought, cause a drop in standards – indeed, quite the reverse. North Western bore this out – for example, I cannot think of more comfortable seats on a service bus of any period than were standard on that company's buses of the 'thirties.

By the time I began travelling on them, J. W. Womar junior was already in the Army, determined to pursue an engineering slant from his initial application to become an officer cadet – that side of the business had already appealed most to him in a junior role with North Western. He spent much of the war in North Africa and Italy, responsible for ensuring that fleets of tanks were in good fighting trim despite difficult conditions, including those created by enemy action, and yet finding that bus company methods would adapt to military needs.

The converse was also true, and Walter belongs to that generation whose whole lives were greatly influenced by the combination of a disciplined approach and yet human comradeship of wartime experience, notably how to deal with people, an art by no means always properly understood today. The wartime chapters in this account often provide the key to later episodes, not least because of the nursing sister he met as a patient in a field hospital in 1943 and married in 1944 – Helen's story, reproduced as one of the appendices, is almost a book in itself.

Yet the return to civilian life was certainly no bed of roses and if the wartime dangers had gone, so had the status that had been earned by wartime promotions – as Helen puts it, 'we were now the lowest of the low' despite Walter being a BET group management trainee, based with Maidstone & District.

Gradually, steps up the ladder came, although involving a succession of moves, the first, in 1949, being to the Northern and associated companies based in Gatehead, where Walter found himself involved in an anti-nationalisation campaign and then the replacement of BET's last street tramway by buses. Association with a variety of types of vehicle – trams, buses, tanks, buses again – was to prove a feature of J.W.W.'s career, with even a spell as Chief Engineer of a fleet of steam and diesel road rollers and other road-making machinery for Eddison Plant. Then it was back to buses with Potteries Motor Traction and the first General Manager post for J. W. W. 'junior' with that same company before the move to Midland Red.

By that time, there were fresh problems with which to contend, perhaps most obviously the vast increase in car ownership. In the 'sixties, this was strongest of all in the Midlands and it was ironic that the busy factories that gave Midland Red plenty of business carrying their workers were also, in effect, beginning to undermine the company in two ways. Shortages of staff caused by tempting wages in the car industry led to unreliability of service and, at the same time, more cars being put on the road, tempting more potential passengers from the buses.

There were political troubles too, with a renewed threat of nationalisation – always anathema to Walter – and among my first memories of him was in travelling to Birmingham to report on protest meetings which he had organised. Relationships between the big company fleets belonging to the BET and Tilling combines and independent concerns were not always very good, but the extrovert Womar way plus a sense of common purpose worked wonders and a very effective liaison was built up, not least with Ron Whittle of what nowadays is called Go Whittle, for whom Walter soon developed much respect.

As Walter conveys in the text, the decision by BET to sell out to the State-owned Transport Holding Company came as a great shock, quite apart from the embarassment of the Midland Red coaches which were carrying anti-nationalisation slogans and running into Victoria Coach Station – I recall that it took a little while for the lettering to disappear!

Yet, despite the nationalised status under which Midland Red and its General Manager then found themselves as part of the National Bus Company, the most acute problem they experienced was the strictly commercial one of making ends meet, under the classic pincer movement of falling traffic and rising costs. How that was overcome was to indicate the path that other NBC subsidiaries and indeed the industry as a whole were soon also to follow. Visits to Midland Red to learn how this and other problems were being tackled were always fruitful in providing the basis of articles with plenty of substance in them.

Later, changes of career caused our paths to cross less frequently for a time, Walter moving to NBC headquarters in London in 1972 when he was appointed an executive Director of that organisation. Now and again, I would see him when he was attending a meeting at Sardinia House, the headquarters of the Confederation of British Road Passenger Transport, better known in those days as CPT, of which I was a member of staff by then, sometimes looking back on those earlier, perhaps more exciting, times.

Hence, soon after the idea of this book being written was first proposed, I was particularly happy to become involved. I was convinced from the start that a life so full of incident would make a good story. Subsequent conversations with Walter would trigger positive torrents of fresh memories, recounted with great gusto and by no means in chronological order as one story would lead to another.

At first there seemed to be an almost overwhelming mass of recollections, but it soon became clear that there were threads which linked it all together, punctuated by the decisive turning points which led to the choice of title. I have thoroughly enjoyed helping to get so varied a story into print. An important aspect of all this was the revelation that, despite Walter's lifelong support for the Conservatives and strong belief in the merits of private enterprise, he does not subscribe to some of the dogma favoured in recent years. In particular he is far from happy with the concept of deregulation and the continual instability and inadequate fleet renewal it appears to imply, as conveyed in the chapter headed 'Some wrong turnings'. Perhaps the politicians, of whatever persuasion, should heed such warnings from someone with a lifetime's experience in transport.

Alan Townsin
Steventon

ACKNOWLEDGEMENTS

In an autobiography like this, acknowledgements fall into two categories. One covers the countless people who helped me in my way through my life, and the other those more directly concerned with the book itself.

Among the former, it would never be possible to name all, even among those to whom I feel I owe a great deal, though many are mentioned in the text. Particularly In Army days, sometimes fate would throw people together in situations of close loyalty to each other, briefly, and then send them in different directions, never to meet again. So I won't attempt a list which would be bound to be far from complete.

In regard to the book itself, I was encouraged from the beginning by my dear wife Helen and daughter Jackie. The same applies to Bob Bailey, who provided many helpful notes stretching back to the beginnings of the close friendship of our two families when we both worked for Northern General and again later with PMT, some of which I have incorporated within the story – I am sad that he did not live to see the finished product. Other former colleagues to whom I am grateful for encouragement are John Nunneley, who was in charge of British Transport Advertising when I was NBC's representative on its Board, and Tony West, whose public relations expertise was so valuable at Midland Red.

The account of the battle of Hammam-Lif which appears as Appendix I is only part of the assistance and support given by Lt-Col A. K. Waterston. I am also grateful for the help of George Martin, whose photographs of life with the 2nd Lothians help to convey a little of the atmosphere of those days, and to R. A. Whitehead for pictures and historical information on Eddison Plant. Some of the tram pictures were obtained via the Tramway Museum Society with the help of Geoffrey Hyde, other pictures came from Geoff Atkins, Alan B Cross, A E Jones, Roy Marshall and David Waymann, in addition to those from the extensive collections of John Senior and Alan Townsin.

The idea of turning my story into a book sprang from contact with John Senior – indeed this volume wouldn't have existed but for his valuable advice and encouragement. Quite a bit of the text was captured from tapes of long conversations we had. Inevitably, one memory would trigger another and the good ladies transcribing them at Glossop had to struggle with drafts which might jump from buses in the Midlands in the 'sixties to the Army in North Africa in 1943 and back again.

Then Alan Townsin came into the picture, and of course we'd known each other from the days when he came to visit me at Midland Red. There was a strong sense of mutual understanding, partly stemming from several parallels in our lives, which helped in the further process of meetings, correspondence and telephone calls during which the text gradually emerged into what we both hope is a readable account, inevitably bringing back more memories as the process continued. Finally, the expertise at 128 Pikes Lane turned it all into the finished product ready to print and I would like particularly to mention Margaret Davies, who had worked on those early tapes as well as more recent text and the layout stages, and Carolyn Senior dealing with the illustrations.

Chapter One: My early life

Life, in my opinion, is often about turning points and grasping any opportunities that may come along. The story of my career, following on from my father's, covers over 80 years, mainly in the bus industry, interrupted by two world wars. My father, also J. W. Womar, his Christian names being James William, started at the age of fourteen as a tramways parcels boy and myself, James Walter Womar, at sixteen as an engineering apprentice. We both finished up as Chairmen of bus companies, learning much about successful management on the way, some of which will, I hope, be passed on by this book. My father's career had begun in June 1908, when he took a job as parcels boy with the Hartlepool Electric Tramways Company Limited. This was one of many tramway undertakings which were part of the group run by the British Electric Traction Company Limited. The BET concern, which was to play an important part in both my father's life and my own over a period of almost 60 years, had been founded in 1896 by Emile Garcke with the objective of building up a chain of tramway undertakings covering suitable routes in many parts of the country. They used the then recently developed form of electric motive power with a central power supply conveyed by overhead wires from which the traction motors on the trams drew the current via trolley arms – hence the company's name. BET also became involved in electric power generation. The Hartlepool company was one of many subsidiaries with their own power stations. In later years, BET diversified as well as switching from electric trams to motor buses

and is still an important company today, even though no longer primarily engaged in the provision of public transport.

The operation of a parcel collection and delivery service was one of the activities of the Hartlepool company, like many others in the group, and my father's first job was the provision of this in the area of Seaton Carew, terminus of one of the tram routes operated in that town, situated north of the River Tees on the coast of County Durham. Before long, however, he was able to gain experience of all branches of the business-traffic, electrical distribution, rolling stock and permanent way. As stores clerk and traffic clerk he took part in the valuation, both for the company and the corporation when, in 1912, West Hartlepool Corporation decided to purchase the system.

This was quite a common procedure at the time, as legislation gave municipalities the option of taking over company-operated tramways operating within their areas, usually after 21 years, and often on very favourable terms. The entire staff of the company, with the single important exception of the General Manager, Mr George Cardwell, transferred to the Corporation. In 1913, my father, still only nineteen, was promoted to chief clerk by Mr Charles Burgess, who had been appointed as manager following the transfer to the Corporation. George Cardwell stayed with BET and was transferred to Devonport, where the combine had another tramway company. He remained in touch and was to play a big part in my father's life and hence mine, as will be seen

The Hartlepools were on the receiving end of a brutal demonstration of wartime dangers just over four months after the outbreak of the 1914-18 war, when the German navy bombarded the area on 16th December 1914, and my father was among the casualties, though fortunately only receiving a cut head. This hit on a Baptist chapel at Hartlepool made one of a series of dramatic subjects for the local postcard trade.

Not all the shells fired from the German battle cruisers performed their intended destruction and this photograph, taken on 16th December 1914, shows two which, mercifully, failed to explode.

BOMBARDMENT OF HARTLEPOOLS, DEC. 16. 1914. UNEXPLODED SHELLS FIRED BY THE GERMAN BATTLE CRUISERS

later. Meanwhile, however, my father's duties made him responsible to Mr Burgess for the whole of the clerical and commercial work of the tramways department. This gave him a good knowledge of traffic regulation and control. Dad said he owed Mr Burgess more than any other chief for whom he ever worked.

However, the outbreak of war with Germany in August 1914 brought major changes. This was more dramatic than mere problems of staff and material shortage, for on 16th December that year, the German Navy bombarded the Hartlepools area and the Corporation's offices were seriously damaged. My father suffered a cut head but was so busy sorting out cash and tickets from the debris that it was two days before he got to a doctor.

Then at the age of 21 he joined the Durham (Fortress) Royal Engineers for the duration of the war, although he was transferred to 595th (Tees) Fortress Company, Royal Engineers, in 1918, being promoted company quartermaster sergeant. Married by then, he was actually

on a troopship about to sail to France in March 1918 when I was born and managed somehow to get compassionate leave. As it turned out, few of those troops were to return home, so he always said that I saved his life.

My mother had a sister in Horsforth, Leeds, which seemed a safer place than the Hartlepool area, and so I was born there and can thus claim to be a Yorkshireman by birth. However, we returned to West Hartlepool and my father returned to the Corporation when demobilised after the end of the war in November 1918. This took a little time, as he was on headquarters staff in the Army and responsible for assisting in demobilising of others before himself, and then on arrival at his former employers had to wait until the General Manager returned from the forces before he could resume his former position, which had been filled by an acting chief clerk in his absence.

By 1921, he thought it was time to look for advancement elsewhere. By then he had a wife and three children to support. I was too young to remember much about West Hartlepool beyond a mental picture of going under a bridge on top of an open-topped tram. But my father's life, and mine, were about to leave the world of trams for buses. George Cardwell got in touch with my dad to say he had a vacancy for a chief clerk at Macclesfield in Cheshire.

BET had created a subsidiary company, the British Automobile Development Co Ltd, in 1905 with the object of building up motor bus operation. The title was changed to British Automobile Traction Co Ltd in 1912 to avoid the unfortunate initials of the original name. Branches were established in various locations, and one of those chosen had been Macclesfield, where Mr Sidney Garke, son of the BET founder, carried out a survey in 1913. The general principle was that BAT would open up motor bus services in areas where no BET tramway was in operation and which were thought suitably promising. There had been a proposal for the seeking of

My father, James William Womar, in army uniform, probably not very long after he joined up, though he had acquired a lance-corporal's stripes.

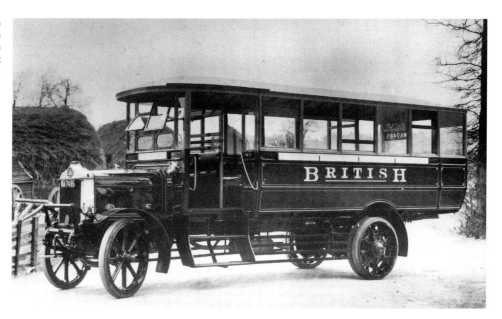

This dark green British bus, registered in Cheshire, operated from Macclesfield. An AEC, it carried Brush bodywork.

powers to operate a BET tramway in Crewe, by then an important railway centre, about 20 miles away, in 1903, but this had not been pursued and so the first BET venture in the area was BAT's Macclesfield-Crewe service begun in 1913. The Daimler buses were painted in BAT's then usual green livery and carried the fleetname "British". Services to Leek, Buxton and Cheadle were soon added.

George Cardwell had been appointed General Manager of the Macclesfield branch of BAT on his release from army service. In 1919 he continued the process of expansion, and approached my father in 1921, offering the position of chief clerk of the branch. However, this meant a considerable drop in salary, from £350 to £250 per year. He decided to accept it, largely on the basis that the future seemed likely to lie with buses rather than trams. This proved to be so, yet at that date the electric tram was still dominant as the main form of public transport in most major British cities and towns. My father took up his new appointment on 1st

George Cardwell, for whom my father had worked at Hartlepool and who sent for him to become chief clerk in 1921, when expanding the BAT branch at Macclesfield. Their careers remained in step after the formation of the North Western Road Car Co Ltd in 1923, of which Mr Cardwell became the first General Manager.

July 1921, noting at the time that the business had 23 buses and five charabancs. An important step taken that year was the start of services in Stockport, where a garage and workshop for three vehicles was opened by converting two cottages, and an office was rented in Mersey Square where waste land was used as a terminus. Briefly the branch was operated under a special sub-committee of the BAT board, known as the Peak District Committee.

Thomas Tilling Ltd, with a history largely based on horse-bus operation in London, had emerged as another strong force in the development of motor bus operation in various parts of the country. It took a sizeable shareholding in BAT in 1922 and in April 1923 the Peak District Committee activities of BAT were taken over by a newly-formed company, the North Western Road Car Co Ltd, of which Tilling and BAT each held 50 per cent of the capital. George Cardwell was appointed General Manager and my father was appointed Secretary. The registered office was at first still in Macclesfield, but the new North Western fleetname was adopted along with a change of livery to red and white. The shade was quite closely akin to that adopted by both Stockport and Manchester Corporation for their trams and buses, a clear indication of growing interest in the urban area extending into the city of Manchester. Yet the new company was also expanding into the more outlying areas. The fleet had grown to 51 at the time of its formation and 60 were in stock by the end of the year.

It was decided to build a new garage, workshop and offices in Charles Street, Stockport, and these became the headquarters from 1924. My father was given the additional duty of Chief Traffic Superintendent that year. The Tilling influence on the company was strong at this time, and in fact the direct and indirect Tilling shareholding was such that the company was under Tilling control until 1942. In 1928, BAT was reconstructed, becoming Tilling and British Automobile Traction Ltd and, in 1929, North Western was one of many bus companies in which the railway companies acquired a shareholding equal to that of TBAT, in this case being split between the London Midland & Scottish and the London & North Eastern Railways.

Expansion during the 'twenties was rapid. The first rival business to be acquired was the Mid-Cheshire Motor Bus Co Ltd of Northwich, and its 20-vehicles business was taken over in November 1924. A larger neighbouring company, the Crosville Motor Co Ltd, based in Chester, had also been interested but George Cardwell and my father beat them to it. The following year, however, an agreement was made with Crosville, in those days an independent company, which established an agreed boundary running south-west of Warrington beyond which neither company would stray into the territory of the other and a similar agreement was made soon afterwards with another concern, Lancashire United Transport Ltd, operating to the north of the Manchester-Warrington road. Gradually, agreements were made with operators in all surrounding areas, many of which were associated because of the railway interest, quite apart from those concerns in which the Tilling and BET companies held interests either through Tilling & British Automobile Traction or otherwise – similar patterns were developing in most other parts of the country.

It should be explained that, in general, direct competition was the order of the day at that time, and in most cases smaller competitors eventually sold out whilst larger ones arrived at agreements as mentioned in the previous paragraph. Municipalities were in a different category, for they often exercised licensing powers within their territory, especially where they were operating their own passenger services, usually in the form of tramways. North Western followed a policy of making agreements where it could and gradually they were signed with the municipalities of Warrington, Oldham, Manchester and Stockport.

While all this was going on, my father's responsibilities grew as the company did. By 1929 he had become Assistant General Manager and when George Cardwell was invited to join Thomas Tilling Ltd at its London headquarters in 1930, my father was appointed General Manager. By then, there were garages at Altrincham, Buxton, Glossop, Macclesfield, Northwich, Oldham and Urmston as well as the Stockport headquarters, and one was being opened in Manchester. Fleet expansion had been rapid, with 90 new Tilling-Stevens Express B10 type single-deckers, lower built than their predecessors, purchased in 1928, and 80 more in 1929, following earlier batches of the same make. Almost the entire fleet consisted of Tilling-Stevens vehicles, apart from a few buses from taken-over businesses. This reflected the Tilling interest in the Tilling-Stevens concern, although this was about to be ended – earlier examples were of the petrol-electric type, but conventional gearboxes had been standard since 1927.

Meanwhile I was growing up. Dad insisted that we first went to an ordinary council school, among working-class people, so that later in life one would see both sides of any situation, as he had done. Later, I went to Stockport Grammar School, where I did not do particularly well, not being of an academic nature.

By the early 1930s I was old enough to begin to take an interest in what my father did and hence in the North Western company and its activities. Yet I was more interested at that stage in the vehicles themselves and how they worked. When Dad became General Manager, we had a chauffeur called Radcliffe and I remember helping him to decarbonise the engine of the Lanchester 18hp car we had – I would be about fourteen years old at the time. I have never been one of those people who wanted to go out on bicycles or, later, in cars, and was much more interested in how things worked and the processes of servicing or repair.

Common Sense

In those days, it was normal to remove cylinder heads of engines to scrape off carbon deposits and regrind valves quite frequently and one day while we were busy with this he said to me, "Walter, what we are doing now is common sense." This idea of what engineering is about, basically, implanted itself on my mind and had the effect of leading to my decision that I wanted to be an engineer. It was not that he or anyone else persuaded me – indeed my Dad was not keen on the idea. He brought all sorts of people in other walks of life, such as auditors, and other professions, round to the house for a meal so that I could listen to them, in the hope that I would change – to no avail.

We lived in Bramhall, a few miles from Stockport, where I went to the Grammar School as well as, later, to the Technical College, and of course where the North Western Road Car headquarters and workshops were situated. Family life tended to revolve round transport depot visits, though I remember how Mum used to like to have a picnic near the proverbial babbling brook.

Dad paid numerous visits to other operating companies and manufacturers and if I was not at school, I would go with him. There were snooker, billiards, football or other sports competitions between the various companies, so that provided a reason for many such trips, though in any case he liked to keep in touch.

The passing of the Road Traffic Act of 1930, by then in force, altered the relationship with other operators considerably, as it introduced the road service licensing system administered via the Traffic Commissioners, putting bus operation on a more secure footing. In general, a newcomer would not be granted a licence for a service directly competing with one already established, and thus existing operators, large or small, could plan with a greater degree of confidence. On the other hand, fares increases, also subject to Traffic Commissioners approval, would not be granted unless justification for them could be demonstrated in detail, and major operators were expected to accept that they had a duty to provide some services that did not pay as part of a general network. There were not many independent operators of bus services still in business in the North Western company's area, but several of these were subsequently taken over by acquisition. In general, relationships with

North Western standardised on Tilling-Stevens buses during its earlier years, and this Express B10A2 model was typical of 325 examples of the model dating from 1928-32. It was No. 555 (DB 9455) with Brush bodywork, placed in service in 1931 but looking much as built when seen here in Lower Mosley Street bus station, Manchester, in May 1935 – note the bunting evident for the Silver Jubilee of King George V and Queen Mary.

the surviving independent concerns were very friendly, in line with the general philosophy of my father and George Cardwell before him.

The North Western fleet had become almost completely standardised on Tilling-Stevens buses, beginning with a delivery of 30 of the petrol-electric TS6 model in 1924, but from 1927 versions with conventional crash gearboxes were adopted and from 1928 there were large deliveries of the Tilling-Stevens Express B10A series of chassis already mentioned, the 80 of 1929 being followed by 81 in 1930, 62 in 1931 and a final dozen in 1932. This model was a well-tried simple design, with four-cylinder side-valve petrol engine of 5.1 litres capacity, and it is of interest that my father is on record as saying in 1932 ''I have yet to be convinced that any more than four cylinders are necessary for stage carriage services''. The occasion of that remark was the 1932 Institute of Transport Congress, held in Buxton and including a visit to North Western's headquarters in Stockport. The fleet at that time consisted of 383 vehicles, all but 43 of which were of Tilling-Stevens make, as indicated, the remainder being quoted as Leyland, including some recently delivered six-cylinder Tiger coaches and a batch of six Titan TD1 double-deckers dating from 1931. Various other makes had been represented among vehicles acquired with businesses taken over in the 1920s but these had been sold off by then.

At that stage, the Tilling-Stevens buses were still fitted with their original bodywork by Tilling and Brush. In those days the bodybuilding works of Thomas Tilling Ltd in London supplied many of that concern's associated companies, while the Brush Electrical Engineering Co Ltd tended to be favoured by BET associates. The link of Tilling with Tilling-Stevens ended in 1930, the latter company's position as the main supplier to operating companies under Tilling control being taken over by the Bristol concern which came into

the Tilling empire in 1931, though Bristol buses did not begin to arrive in most associated fleets until a few years later, 1936 in the case of North Western.

In the meantime, new deliveries were split between Dennis and Leyland chassis, the Dennis Lancet model with four-cylinder petrol engine being favoured for 30 single-deckers in 1934. They had bodywork built almost to coach standards by Eastern Counties Omnibus Co Ltd. This latter was another associated company controlled by Tilling, which had been formed in 1931 and in addition to operating bus services in East Anglia, took over the Lowestoft based-bodybuilding works originally established by United Automobile Services Ltd. It had built the bodies on a batch of 25 Leyland Tiger TS4 coaches for North Western in 1932, and Eastern Counties' bodybuilding department, later reformed as a separate company, Eastern Coach Works Ltd, was to supply most of the bus bodywork for North Western for the rest of the 'thirties, though Thomas Harrington Ltd of Hove got most of the contracts for coach bodywork.

A noteworthy development was the rebodying of 158 of the Tilling-Stevens B10A buses with up-to-date Eastern Counties or Eastern Coach Works bodies beginning in 1935. Not only was there reason to visit the various firms mentioned, but also suppliers of components or materials. Among these were John Holdsworth & Co Ltd of Halifax, a company which produced moquette for bus seats. Visits were also made to other firms and I recall that dad got on well with the boss of a bodybuilding firm in Leeds, which seems almost certain to have been Charles H Roe of the firm of the same name, even though not a supplier. The Gardner engine works at Patricroft was within the company's operating area, as well as being a supplier, although the letter did not apply until 1936 and hence comes into the story a little later.

Chapter Two: North Western Road Car 1934-39

Gradually, as I grew older, I became more involved with the activities of the North Western Road Car Co Ltd, where my father continued as General Manager. Even before officially becoming part of the staff, I found myself taking part in the social contacts which formed an important part of the life of a firm in which team spirit was important, as in all well-run bus companies.

Then I began as an apprentice in the company's Stockport workshops, with a wage of 10 shillings (50p) per week, which included Saturday mornings, with one-day release to the Stockport Technical College, which I also attended for two evenings per week.

I was only about seventeen-and-a-half and had not long learned to drive. George Brook, then the company's Secretary, and Bill Leese, then Traffic Assistant, both of whom were, successively, to become General Manager of the company in later years, were going the hilly route over the Pennines to Halifax to play in a snooker competition. A Morris Cowley car owned by the firm at the time, and not in its first youth, was being used and I was taken along for reasons which were explained.

"Whatever happens when we come out, we'll have had a few drinks and you're to drive, regardless". Anyway, when the match was over, and as the three of us climbed into the front seat there was only a front seat – George Brook said "I'm driving". "Oh, well" I thought, "he's driving", and we set off. We got a little part of the

My father at his desk in North Western's Charles Street, Stockport, headquarters – he was General Manager between 1930 and 1946.

way and the gear lever broke off – not for the only time in my career, by the way. So we were stuck in whatever gear it was, fortunately low enough to get over the hills and dales, and George said 'Walter, you take over" – nothing new in that, either.

So I took over the wheel, and we were about half-way home. It was about two o'clock in the morning, and I realised we were climbing quite a steep hill which was also a one-way street, but it was the wrong way! So I said "What do I do now?" "For Christ's sake keep going, Walter". So I did and we struggled home, still in low gear, all the way.

Talking of hills, I should mention my Dad's idea to save fuel still petrol at that stage – on the company's buses. In those days, it was quite common practice for drivers to coast – allowing the vehicle to roll along with the gear lever in neutral or the clutch pedal depressed. In a hilly area such as most of North Western's terrain, there were plenty of places where this could be done, although also plenty where it was risky.

My father's plan was to have a bonus scheme based on comparisons of fuel consumption between depots. The aim was to reduce costs and the drivers entered into the spirit of it, coasting for considerable distances and down hills because they were all trying to get this bonus. The only trouble was that it led to the burning out of brake linings and even caused some accidents. It was an initiative that really didn't work out as planned, but illustrates the adventurous attitude of those days. The idea was dropped, and indeed, such behaviour would have been frowned upon very severely only a few years later.

However, before I re-joined my father's firm, I was sent to Leyland Motors Ltd for a spell as an apprentice in 1938, the idea being to gain an insight into engineering methods at a major manufacturer. My time there included spells in the drawing office and working on oil engines, as we used to call diesel engines in those days. By that date almost all buses built at Leyland were oil-engined, even though regular production of such units had not begun until about 1932, numbers remaining small until the big swing-over from petrol in 1933-35. The General Manager was A. A. Liardet, another of the personalities my father knew well.

By that date, the North Western fleet had lost its earlier emphasis on Tilling-Stevens models, though the 158 Express B10 series models rebodied by Eastern Counties and Eastern Coach Works (to the distinctive company style with half-canopy cab and rear entrance) still formed the largest group of single-deckers. As well as the Dennis Lancet buses mentioned in the previous chapter, deliveries had begun in 1936 of Bristol chassis,

By 1934, when I joined the firm as an apprentice, vehicle design had advanced considerably. This Leyland Tiger TS6, No.662, freshly in service when photographed by Geoff Atkins in Nottingham in August of that year, had Harrington bodywork representative of the latest ideas on coach design. A Barton Leyland Lion LT5 and Nottingham Corporation trolleybus can also be seen.

Harrington's half-canopy cab style of the 1934 coaches was adopted as standard for North Western's single-deckers generally from 1935. The bodywork was built at Lowestoft by Eastern Counties and then Eastern Coach Works, the latter being represented by this Bristol JO5G, No.729, dating from 1936, and also seen in Nottingham, awaiting departure on the express service to Manchester. It was one of the first batch of Bristol vehicles for the fleet, beginning a long association of North Western with the make.

beginning with batches of 24 and then 50 of the JO5G model that year. Leyland chassis were favoured for coaches, the earlier Tiger TS4 and TS6 petrol models being followed by batches of TS7 and TS8 models, latterly with the smooth-running 8.6-litre oil engine of that period, and having Harrington bodywork. In fact it had been the Harrington half-canopy that had been copied for use on subsequent ECOC and then ECW single-deck bus bodies for North Western in 1935.

When I returned to North Western in 1938, deliveries were beginning of the latest series of Bristol model, including an initial batch of twelve of the double-deck K5G and 50 of the single-deck L5G. The double-deckers replaced six 1931 Leyland Titan TD1 models which had been the only double-deckers in the fleet in the mid-'thirties, but the double-deck strength was to grow steadily, a second dozen K5G models arriving before the end of the year and 40 more in 1939. All of these had Eastern Coach Works lowbridge bodies of the style then being supplied to several of the associated company fleets, but North Western's interior was quite

different, with coach-style seats for only 47 passengers.

The use of luxurious seating was company policy at the time, all the above-mentioned single-deckers, plus a further 45 L5G buses delivered later in 1938 and a final eleven in 1940, had the same style of coach seats for 31 passengers apiece.

All the Bristol buses had the Gardner 5LW five-cylinder oil engine which, if rather noisy and prone to vibration, was proving exceptionally reliable and economical on fuel, without any need for risky coasting down hills. The JO5G and L5G buses had five-speed overdrive gearboxes which played an important part in this – the average fuel consumption they were returning over the first eight months of 1939 was 13.9 miles per gallon, whilst the Bristol K5G double-deckers were almost as impressive at 12.66 mpg. Anyone who knows the area covered by North Western in those days, including many hilly routes, could not fail to be impressed. Modern vehicles are larger, heavier and more powerful, but such fuel economy is remarkable, even by the best standards of half-a-century later.

My father had quite strong ideas about comfort, even passengers on local North Western services being provided with coach-like seating and trim; the seating capacity was standardised at 31 to suit. This is the interior of another 1936 Bristol JO5G with ECW body, No.755, but by 1939 virtually the whole fleet offered similar standards – even the double-deckers had this type of seat. Maybe some of today's bus designers could learn a thing or two about attracting people from their cars from this example of nearly 60 years ago.

In my own position as a technical assistant. I reported to Warwick Wroth, who was Chief Engineer, and another of the people I first knew in those days at North Western whom I was to meet again 20 years later in my career.

It was a period of valuable experience, not only in being able to observe how an efficiently-run bus and coach undertaking was controlled at all levels and learning not only about the mechanical side of keeping a fleet of buses on the road but also about people and how to deal with them. Like many bus companies established in the early days of mechanical road transport, it had great esprit-de-corps of a kind not dissimilar to that I was soon to find in the Army. There was a sense of pride and this extended to the vehicles – a scruffy North Western bus was unheard of, and this was still evident when I returned at the end of the war. A small handful of the fleet was in wartime grey paint, but this was virtually confined to the utility buses built under wartime restrictions, and the remainder was still in the traditional red and white, the latter by no means easy to keep clean in a largely industrial area, yet somehow it, and the proper repair of vehicles to keep them smart and efficient, had been achieved.

When war came, on 3rd September 1939, a new chapter of my life was about to begin, as I shall recount in the next chapter of this volume. However, one further aspect of the story of my father and North Western deserves mention. He had always be keen on adequate welfare arrangements to look after the staff. He was known as the 'Bear' because he was firm but fair in his approach and this continued right up to the war. The trade unions had made little if any impact and I think North Western was possibly the last major operating company, certainly in a largely urban area, to remain out of the union's clutches.

However, when the wartime coalition Government under Winston Churchill was formed after Britain found itself virtually alone in 1940, Ernest Bevin was appointed Minister of Labour. He had been leader of the Transport and General Workers Union before the war,

and involved in many major disputes involving busmen, notably in London. In his new job, he was well suited to harnessing the nation's labour force to the war effort, and widely recognised as one of the great war leaders. It was inevitable that the trade unions were brought into the picture to a greater extent.

I must explain at this point that in 1942 it was decided to split the very complex Tilling and British Automobile Traction group to which North Western belonged into two completely separate Tilling- and BET-owned parts. The Tilling and BET ways of running things were very different, something which was to become evident again in 1968 when the two groups' bus companies came together and the National Bus Company was set up, as I shall explain more full later. Tilling, under the chairmanship of Frederick Heaton – he was knighted during the war – was run on very centralised lines, such matters as vehicle policy being closely controlled from headquarters.

On the other hand, BET allowed individual operating companies a fair degree of discretion, even though there were strong centralised services available from its headquarters, too. It was to BET that North Western was transferred in the 1942 split, somewhat to everyone's surprise, as it had been under Tilling influence as part of TBAT. The chairmanship of BET was in the hands of R. J. Howey in those days, but much of the day-to-day management was carried out by John Spencer Wills, a remarkable man who had begun as personal assistant to BET's founder, Emile Garcke, and became Secretary of East Yorkshire Motor Services Ltd on its foundation in 1926 at the age of 22, rising rapidly to become a main board director of BET only thirteen years later. It fell to John Spencer Wills, I believe, to send a message from BET headquarters to my father – "Well, there is a war on, you will just have to get on with it now" – and so the unions came in.

However, while this was happening, I was far away from the world of buses, even though what I had learnt about them and how to deal with people was to prove useful, as I will tell in the next chapter.

Chapter Three: The 1939-45 War – I become a soldier

The outbreak of war with Germany on 3rd September 1939 was a turning point for millions of lives, and it was certainly one of the most important in mine. Yet although there were to be huge and dramatic changes, there was a strand of continuity, for what I had already learned in my career, short even though it was at that stage, about looking after a bus fleet was to prove a key part of the basis for my war service, largely devoted to keeping about 70 tanks and support vehicles in top fighting trim and, later, broader responsibility for many more. Then, when the war was over, what I learned about men and leadership, as well as coping with mechanical problems under extreme stress was to prove invaluable in my subsequent career.

However, it was by no means straightforward at the beginning. Simply getting into a role within the armed forces that would make use of my engineering knowledge was to prove far from easy, yet I felt determined that this was the right thing to do. I was 21 years old when the war broke out. There had been ideas that I should go to Manchester University – which would not have suited me at all – but when hostilities began, I was pursuing two opportunities for obtaining a commission, one in the Royal Army Service Corps, which was responsible for the Army's transport, and the other in the Royal Air Force on the transport side.

I was accepted for both but there were waiting lists, and before I could take advantage of either I was called up at the end of December 1939. The intention was that I should go to the Cheshire regiment, appropriately enough, for that was the county in which I lived, though quite a high proportion of those called up were posted to regiments very far from home. I was to be trained as a machine gunner when, to the disgust of the Colonel, I got a transfer to a Royal Army Ordnance Corps supply depot at Burscough in Lancashire as a driver and later driver mechanic.

I became a member of a Light Aid Detachment doing repair work in Sennybridge, South Wales. The LAD units provided a specialist service to augment and oversee the normal regimental maintenance routine, tackling work that was beyond the scope of troops whose training could only include simple servicing of tanks and other vehicles. They were part of the RAOC rather than the regiment to which they were attached, moving with the latter to carry out their duties under active service conditions and, if need be, under enemy attack, getting disabled vehicles back into service if possible. Later, with the formation of the Royal Mechanical and Electrical Engineers in 1943, the LADs became part of that organisation.

Historically, the development of the tank as a self-propelled track-borne fighting vehicle, and also of the armoured car, generally rather smaller and on wheels rather than tracks, had resulted in their operation by cavalry regiments. Even today, some regiments combine ceremonial duties with horses with their function as fighting units based on tanks. The LAD units were attached to these fighting regiments and played a vital role in keeping in readiness, as indeed they still do, as proved by experiences in the Gulf War in 1991.

At first, the outbreak of war was something of an anti-climax. We had been led to expect almost immediate heavy air attacks, and indeed the atmosphere of an impending end to almost all that was normal affected most walks of life in one way or another. Back at home, the North Western company, like many bus fleets, had been asked to convert a number of single-deckers – six,

I had my name on waiting lists for two commission courses when I was called up and found myself as Pte Womar, J.W., in the Cheshire Regiment – I was thus in much the same situation as my father 25 years earlier. It was not easy to look smart in an Army-issue greatcoat – this photograph was taken in Blackpool in 1940.

as far as I can recall – to act as ambulances, the seats being removed and racks to take stretchers fitted. Access was from the rear, an opening at the rear with black curtaining being provided to give easy access for rapid loading of casualties.

The black-out was enforced immediately, with drastically reduced output from, at first, only one heavily masked headlamp per vehicle and even the sidelights reduced in output, creating great difficulties in driving after dark. Inside, lighting was made very dim and conductors had similar difficulty in dealing with change – inevitably, some people tried to take advantage.

Volunteers were called upon for air raid duties. A little later in the war, when large numbers of small incendiary bombs began to dropped in air raids, Manchester being one of the cities affected, regular overnight fire-watch duty began to be another part of life, as it had been found that prompt action by quite simple means could often save premises. Bus fleets and garages were regarded as a vital part of the overall transport system. All operation was put under tight restrictions to save fuel, timetables being cut and late night services curtailed.

On a personal level, my brother Bill enlisted in the Royal Air Force and my sister Marjorie was also keen to do her bit for the war effort, so she, like thousands of other women, went to work at an aircraft factory, in this case at Woodford Aerodrome where, later in the war, Avro Lancaster bombers were assembled and tested. She had taken a nursing course, acting as a volunteer at local hospitals. The Womar association with transport recurred in an unusual form as she volunteered for work on the bus ambulances, which were used as a means of transferring patients from trains bringing military or civilian casualties for treatment at the hospitals, among the latter being people transferred from other areas when emergencies caused the need for transfers.

The first few months of the war were relatively quiet, with little more than occasional air raids on coastal towns, except at sea, where attacks on shipping began almost immediately. British troops were sent to France, but saw little action until a major offensive by the German army in the spring and summer of 1940 led to the collapse of France and the evacuation of the British at Dunkirk. Soon, however, the entry of Italy into the war at this stage opened up a new front. Libya, then an Italian colony, posed a potential threat to British interests in the Middle East, most notably the Suez Canal and the oilfields, on which we were then largely dependent for our supplies in Britain and indeed to keep the forces going, in those days long before oil had been found in the North Sea.

Almost the whole of the mainland of Western Europe, apart from neutral countries such as Switzerland, Sweden and Spain (though even the last-mentioned was under a regime friendly to Germany) were by then occupied by what were called the Axis Powers, Germany and Italy. Mounting an invasion against this was clearly going to take time, for the Germans had built up a huge and, thus far, very effective fighting machine.

Thus the Middle East assumed great importance. At first the British Army, already present in fair strength, did well against the Italians, but it soon became clear that this was to be an important theatre of war and both sides were building up major reinforcements. For three years, it was to be the main centre of action for the British Army. The Germans began sending tank divisions to North Africa early in 1941 and gradually what was to be an epic struggle between their Afrika Korps, led by Rommel, and our Eighth Army, at first under Wavell but in the crucial period Montgomery, took shape.

So in 1940, there was I at Tidworth, near Salisbury, as a driver mechanic, almost about to be sent to a ship bound for the Middle East. I had been issued with my topee and the rest of my tropical kit and I'd had my injections. A Colonel had been put in charge of finding the people of a wide range of different trades to fill this ship. I was still keen to get my commission and so I wrote a very special letter to him – I think it amounted to about six pages – I like to convey what I want in one page usually, but this was different. It set out all the reasons I could put together to spell out why it was so important that I should have this commission so as to be able to use my talents properly. I said I would then go anywhere in the world.

By then, I had gained some experience of Army ways, and so I slipped into his office and put the letter on top of the pile of papers in his in-tray, so that it would be the first thing he saw.

Well, he sent for me, bless him, and he said "Womar, I have a ship to fill and I have to have so many driver mechanics. I am very short of them and you are one of them". I said to him "Sir, you read the letter, that's all I can ask you to do. I am very grateful for that". I saluted and turned to leave his office. Just as I was about to go through the door, his phone rang and what turned out to be the vital call in my story came in. It was from Wilton House, Salisbury, which had been General Wavell's headquarters prior to him becoming Commander-in-Chief in the Middle East, and they were looking for a driver. I heard him say "You have no drivers? – it's no good ringing me like that". Then there was a brief pause and he said "Womar". I swung round and he said "Look. Are you prepared and go and have a driving test to see if you would be suitable to drive a Colonel around?" He added, "It means going down from driver mechanic to driver." I simply said "Yes, Sir".

So off I went to Salisbury, praying to God I wouldn't fail the driving test, having learnt to drive in the relaxed ways of the mid 1930s. It was a great big Ford V8, and the Colonel's Personal Assistant to whom I reported was a 2nd Lieutenant, who said "Well, we have to have this driving test." So off we went, and I managed to get through the test without problems. He went up to tell the Colonel, who then interviewed me. He knew I was only in for a few months before I would be sent to an Officer Cadet Training Unit. He accepted me and so all seemed to be settled and I was as happy as a "pig in muck". I went downstairs and there just marching up to the front door was another driver, smartly dressed – I wasn't very

In Britain, civilians took much of the brunt of the earlier part of the war, especially during the heavy bombing suffered from the latter part of 1940 and through 1941. Among the first heavy air raids were those on London in September 1940, when a freak blast effect threw this London Transport STL-type double-decker against a row of houses in Islington. My duties in driving a Colonel around to check on military supply dumps took us all over the country, heading towards wherever we were informed that bombs had fallen.

smart, but he looked a perfect Colonel's driver – he had already been driving for top brass. My heart sank, and the PA said to me "Well, I'm sorry, but here is a chap who is a pukka driver, and you will be gone in a few months' time. Oh dear – I'd better go up and tell the Colonel". However, to that Colonel's eternal credit, he said "I have made my choice", so I got the job. It was to prove a very important turning point in my life.

So in about September 1940 I started on a new and modest-seeming job driving the Colonel. He was in charge of the dumps of military munitions stores – everything from uniforms to shells – that had been laid down in various parts of the country. With the military collapse on the European mainland, it was clear that a strong threat of invasion of Britain had arisen, and at about that time the Germans were indeed preparing to assemble an invasion force to land from the Low Countries, so the safety of material in these dumps and the means of access to them was crucially important. It was vital that any damage or losses due to enemy bombing be evaluated promptly and made up if at all possible.

As it happened, the aerial Battle of Britain was about at its height at the time and Hitler decided to switch the Luftwaffe air attacks, at first concentrated on our airfields, to London. During the following months various other cities and towns were attacked in what became known as the Blitz. In fact that word was derived from the German 'blitzkrieg' which literally meant 'lightning war', intended to refer to the fast-moving type of invasion which had overwhelmed Holland, Belgium and France, but in Britain 'Blitz' was always taken to mean the heavy bombing.

Wherever any bombs dropped, we had to get out straight away and get there as quickly as possible, the Ford V8 being quite a fast car by the standards of the time. We went to Coventry and were there on 14th November 1940, when it suffered one of the most savage bombing attacks made on a British city. We were also there during raids on Portsmouth and Southampton – there were obvious military targets in both cities, notably the naval dockyard in the former and the docks in the

latter, as well as the small but vitally important Supermarine factory where production of the Spitfire fighter planes had begun. Even so, the fact that these places were on the south coast continued to give rise to worry that air raids on them might be a prelude to invasion.

Yet, sometimes there were moments of relaxation. The Colonel was very keen on cathedrals if we were passing nearby – for example to Wells – he would say "Well, Womar, pull over to the left and we'll go and see the cathedral". As a young soldier, I couldn't help thinking "What's this got to do with the war?", for clearly Britain was hard pressed at that stage – but, as it happened, several cathedral cities with little in the way of obvious military targets were quite heavily bombed.

However, one day in March 1941, while I was still driving my Colonel around, we received a telegram. It said "Womar will report to Black Down Forest RASC officers training course", arrived while he was attending a conference. When he came out, I showed him the telegram and, understandably, he said "Well, that's what you wanted, isn't it? That's what you've been driving me around for. Just say 'Yes'". The truth was that it wasn't, and the timing had opened up a much better alternative if only I could achieve it, and as it turned out, luck was again on my side.

It so happened that it was my birthday and at the age of 23 I had just reached I could apply for a commission in the Royal Army Ordnance Corps which would give me what I wanted, which can be summed up as engineering rather than just transport, which was what the RASC offered. I had to reply that day, so I explained to the Colonel. His initial response wasn't encouraging, for he said he thought I was a fool. But I persisted, "If you will arrange an interview with your opposite number in the RAOC, I will take my chance and say 'no' at this moment for this particular thing because I want to be in engineering". He was still unenthusiastic. "Well, I don't know", he said, " you've been all around with me, the Blitz, the lot but, alright, I'll do it".

So he arranged an interview, which was to be in

London and we were going there, as it happened, in any case. I duly arrived looking back, I don't think I made a very good Private, actually, maybe a bit scruffy, even – and I was marched up to this room. However, I was armed with a letter from Hector Tuff, who had proved a true friend – by then he was Chief Engineer with North Western, and understood my ambitions to pursue a similar career as well as teaching me more about the subject. His letter was not only an excellent reference in itself but went so far as to predict that one day I would become a Chief Engineer myself.

The orderly Sergeant took me in and I stood in front of the interviewing officer who fired twenty questions at me. They were on such subjects as how I would operate in the field, how I would manage my staff, and so on. Having been a technical assistant in a bus company meant that in many respects I had been through all that, so it was not as difficult as it would have been without that experience. Even so, I felt very nervous.

At the end, I was ordered to go and stand in the corridor, which I did, while the Orderly Sergeant went in with relevant papers. After a little while he came out and whispered in my ear "God, you've done well". You cannot imagine the relief I felt. So at last I had achieved what I'd hoped, and indeed soon afterwards, duly appointed Lieutenant, I could proudly wear my two pips on each shoulder – another key turning point.

Back in my early days of my army career, while still a Private, I had been under a 2nd Lieutenant Stafford Gaffney – a bit upper-crust, basically alright but perhaps a little fond of his authority – and as I had volunteered to run the stores, and do any administrative work, basically to have something more interesting to do, I was frequently require to do his bidding. I was used to the calls from his little tent – "Womar, do this"...."Womar, do that", and so on.

After being commissioned I had to go back to Tidworth, quite a good camp in those days, for training. I remember felling scared stiff when I arrived and retiring into a corner of the officers' mess to read a book about gas producers. With a shortage of oil, all imported in those days, and subject to submarine attacks on the tankers that brought it, alternative means of running vehicles were important and, back home, North Western was, like all major bus operators, soon to be required to convert part of its fleet to this form of operation. It would be wrong to pretend I was being conscientious, however, for I was really trying to hide my nervousness.

However, when we were called in for dinner, the protocol was that we went in order of seniority of rank, so I got up with the others with two pips in front of those with only one. And who turned out to be among the latter but Stafford Gaffney. He looked at me and said "Oh no, no, you can't be Womar. You must be Womar's brother". "But I am Womar", I assured him as I walked in front of him, with a certain degree of childish delight.

There were more serious tasks to do, however, and I spent some time training an LAD at Newmarket. Fortunately, I was now in a position to begin applying my experience in the methodical maintenance of buses to army circumstances. I came to the conclusion that a system of dealing with one such job every day on a simply-remembered rota basis was best for the conditions to be expected in active service.

It wasn't often that the family were able to get together during the war, but in this picture taken in 1942 before I was posted abroad, I am standing behind my Mum and Dad, with my brother Bill, who was in the RAF, on my right and my sister Marjorie, a nurse, on my left. Car enthusiasts will note the Jaguar saloon my Dad was then running.

Chapter Four: Into battle with the 2nd Lothians

It was not very long before I was reminded of the harsh realities of war. Duly trained in my new duties, once again I was scheduled to go by ship to the Middle East, but this time, in November 1942, we set sail as part of a huge force – altogether there were 650 ships involved, though divided into smaller convoys. We were to make a series of landings to secure a large part of North Africa, then under the control of the Vichy Government of France, which had surrendered to the Germans in 1940. The aim of Operation Torch, as it was called, was to use this base to sweep to the west to attack Rommel's army from the rear. For the first time in the war, it was a joint Anglo-American operation under American overall command, involving large numbers of American troops as well as the British 1st Army, to which I was attached.

Our convoy headed out into the Atlantic at first, rather than cutting across the Bay of Biscay, to try and deceive the enemy of our intention. We were very much aware of the risk of torpedo attack by one of the large numbers of German U-boats known to operate in that area. That didn't happen, but after changing course and as we neared Gibraltar, our ship was in collision in dense fog with a Polish ship. This was less than half the size of ours but suffered less damage, and as our ship was badly holed, we were ordered to clamber over the gang planks with our kit, quite a hazardous business while we were out at sea. For the remainder of the voyage, we had half the already limited space we'd had before.

We went through the straights of Gibraltar into the Mediterranean and eventually landed at Bone, in what was then the French colony of Algeria, shortly after it had been secured. I was attached to the 2nd Lothians and Border Horse Regiment which, as I explained earlier, was originally a cavalry regiment but had converted to tanks. Together with the 16th/5th and 17th/21st Lancers, it formed the 26th Armoured Brigade, part of the 6th Armoured Division of the 1st Army.

The 2nd Lothians 'fleet' for which I was responsible included 70 tanks, initially Valentine and Crusader types, but later including some American-built Shermans and a few of the smaller Honey type, a dozen Daimler armoured cars and various general support vehicles, notably the familiar Bedford 3-tonner. Each of these had their own characteristics and we soon learned both their strengths and weaknesses.

The Valentine was a medium tank, limited in its fighting capability by its small 2-pounder gun. The Crusader was lighter and faster, with a 6-pounder gun, but only had light armour, not capable of withstanding more than small-arms fire. The Sherman was quite tall in build and rather ungainly-looking but was tough, reliable and had a more effective 75mm gun – the arrival of a supply of these effectively saved the day after early battles had shown up the inferiority of the earlier British types when faced with good German tanks. Fortunately the heavier Churchill, when it in turn arrived, helped to even up the balance to some degree.

Most of the various types revealed problems of one kind or another under the tough conditions of service in the desert. Not surprisingly, the sand found its way into oil seals, resulting in failures, notably in the Crusader and the front drive of the Daimler armoured cars. The Bedford lorries suffered from propellor-shaft universal joint failures, while broken valve springs and valves were by no means uncommon, all these faults being also related to the climate, difficult terrain and inevitable hard driving under active service conditions. It has to be said that the manufacturers did try to overcome problems, many of which had not arisen under more normal conditions, and many post-war civilian vehicles benefitted from better air cleaners and more efficient oil seals as a result of wartime experience in North Africa.

The first experience of action came soon after arrival, in December 1942, when the regimental Colonel, Lt-Col D. O' B. E. ffrench Blake, said "We had better show Jerry what we are made of". He was a wonderful man who had ensured, by an intensive programme of training and retraining during the period during the period throughout 1941 and most of 1942 when the regiment was in the Swindon-Marlborough area, that it was brought up to a superb level of efficiency. It seems unbelievable, looking back from today, but there had been no system of maintenance up to the time when I had been posted to take charge of the Light Aid Detachment attached to the regiment, in 1941. His belief in training and my experience of methodical maintenance in a bus company fleet matched up well, and an effective system was put into operation as part of a pattern of training which gave everyone a clear set of duties which could be kept up, even when in action. Lt-Col ffrench Blake was wounded in a subsequent tank battle, recovered, but was killed in a tragic car accident in May 1943, just after the North African campaign was successfully ended.

In those early stages we had the Valentine tank, sometimes described as having pea-shooters on the front because of those ineffective 2-pounder guns. At the time, there was a 'no-man's land' between us and the enemy, who sent out about 21 tanks, moving towards

We were generally too busy for pictures to be taken during the campaign in French North Africa, but in this snapshot I, wearing the beret, am explaining the situation to an American officer during the battle of Fondouk Pass in April 1943, when no less than 75 British 6th Armoured Division tanks were knocked out before we managed to push through the gap towards the sea. The American was a tank expert, particularly in regard to the General Motors diesel engine with which the Shermans were powered.

us and across this area. All Jerry did was to fire one shot through the last tank in our line, almost as if deliberately. It showed that our armour plate was absolutely hopeless, and we had to have great slabs of it sent out from England, which my LAD had to weld on to give the tank crews any worthwhile security. So that wasn't a very bright start.

The next lesson I learned was how difficult it could be to recover the tanks disabled for one reason or another. That had to be done between battles, when the enemy might have had access to them and they were liable to be booby-trapped. We were likely to be told about them when the battle-weary troops were asleep and it wasn't easy to get exhausted men up and out to show where a particular tank had been left or give some indication as to what kind of damage or failure it might have suffered so as to allow us to go out suitably prepared.

About the first occasion I had a significant number of tanks to recover at the same time was rather later in the campaign, about April 1943. I made the very serious mistake of having them all drawn to a tiny village – I think it was El Aroussa, about 50 miles from Tunis, by then our main objective and being fiercely defended by the Germans. There were seven or eight of these tanks, all drawn up neatly in the village square, allowing the mechanics to work on them with tools and equipment readily to hand. As a result, Jerry, probably thinking they were reinforcements, sent over some of his Junkers Ju87 Stuka dive-bombers – the type often seen in newsreel shots – making an awesome screaming sound as they dived and did their best to bomb the hell out of us. I lost my utility car, lost my breakfast and nearly lost my Light Aid Detachment because they were in amongst some ammunition trucks round the corner. That was a real mistake and, provided you survive, you soon learn in war not to do things like that.

However, the episode proved revealing in a quite different respect. Among my team of 21 men was a storeman, seemingly very timid by nature. When the

ammunition trucks were exploding all around, the man who came out of it best in terms of coolness and bravery under fire was this same 'timid' young man. He really rose to the occasion and just took charge, and we were very proud of him. It is quite extraordinary what people will do under extreme stress and great danger – call it hidden strength of will or whatever. I much regret that I cannot remember his name.

I have always found it difficult, yet very important, to detect potential qualities of leadership. It is a key element in deciding who should be chosen for future management, and although finding out what youngsters do in their spare time or holidays may be a useful lead, the episode I have just mentioned shows how an unlikely candidate may have qualities not revealed in normal circumstances.

The plan for exerting pressure on Rommel's Afrika Korps was the classic pincer movement, and had gone very largely as intended. The British 8th Army was pushing westwards from Egypt after the famous victory at Alamein in October 1942, when General Montgomery, as he then was, began to be a national hero. The Operation Torch landings in Morocco and Algeria provided the starting point for the squeeze in the opposite direction, in both cases heading towards Tunis.

In his history 'The Second World War', Winston Churchill gave the volume covering this episode the title 'The Hinge of Fate' and it was the turning point of the war. By the spring of 1943, it drove the entire German and Italian armies in North Africa into a noose and allowed the joining of the British 8th and 1st Armies, putting my own unit under General Montgomery's command.

It is true, by the way, that when Monty addressed gatherings of officers under his command, a box of cough sweets would be passed up and down the rows of seats. When Monty climbed up on to the stage, "Nothing must interrupt what I am going to say to you – there will be no coughing" – and, amazingly, there never was! It was quite remarkable – complete concentration.

(Above) Here, members of 4 Troop, B Squadron, the 2nd Lothians, commanded by Lt. George W. Martin, bareheaded among the group standing in front of a Sherman, representative of many of the tanks for whose fighting efficiency I was responsible. The Sherman was quite tall in profile but its looks were in keeping with its rugged character. These photographs were taken in March 1945, by which time the 2nd Lothians had moved on to Italy, the scene being a training area in Pesaro. George Martin is still in touch and kindly supplied these photographs for reproduction.

(Below) Tank tracks have quite a hard time, especially when operating in abrasive sand or mud, as seen here. Although we attempted to predict life, breakages did occur, as with this Sherman at Pesaro, and the crew or my Light Aid Detachment would be faced with the job of repairing it. This was not an easy task, involving taking up the slack evident in the section running over the sprockets in this view, and although there was time for a smoke here during a training routine at Pesaro, such an event could mean the loss of the tank in battle.

In the final battle for Tunis, the 1st Army, strengthened by three divisions transferred from the 8th Army, made a decisive break-through at a place called Medjez-el-Bab, about 30 miles west of Tunis. Tanks of the 2nd Lothians were involved in this as part of the 6th Armoured Division, and the advance through the Tunis area took a circling movement to the town of Hamman-Lif. Even though the city of Tunis had been taken by then, the Germans had planned to hold the peninsula of Cape Bon, to the east, for long enough to give them chance to regroup, and this little coastal town, which commanded the only route in, was heavily defended. Its capture after two days of intense fighting effectively ended the enemy's hold on the last part of North Africa that remained to them.

The Sherman tanks used in the Hammam-Lif battle were specially waterproofed. We had foreseen the probable need for some of them to be able to carry out a flanking movement by wading along the beach and into the sea, if need be. Clearly it was vital for these tanks to be in prime condition, and the pressure that this should be so laid a heavy responsibility on the LAD, and not least myself.

A graphic account of the action here on 8th/9th May 1943 has been written for me by Lt-Col A. K. Waterston, later to become officer-in-command of the 2nd Lothians & Border Horse, though a lieutenant at the time. It appears as Appendix I but, to summarise very briefly, tanks did indeed wade into the sea and the action almost took on the character of a naval battle, with enemy shells throwing up huge splashes as they hit the water, and an enemy gun position mistaken for a submarine by one participant. After a fierce battle, the town was taken successfully. The driver of another tank in the troop was killed when it was hit and two immediate awards of medals were made for the action, one going to Lieut. Waterston himself, who received the Military Cross for his part.

A pause, and change of role

With the ending of the North African campaign on 12th May, 1943, there was an inevitable pause in the sequence of events, giving time not only to recover and regroup – the 2nd Lothians had lost some 56 officers and men killed in the previous four months. The next stage in the war, so far as that theatre of operations was concerned, was obvious enough – an attack on the European mainland via Italy – but not only did the Army have to be in good order but the type of campaign was bound to be different, with less scope for tanks to manoeuvre freely and more need for close co-operation with infantry.

However, there was a small island, Pantelleria, about halfway between Tunisia and Sicily, which was an obvious stepping stone for what was to follow as well as providing a useful base for air attacks. My LAD team had prepared Sherman tanks for its planned capture about a month later, and I am rather proud to find that their inclusion in the landing force is mentioned in

Winston Churchill's account in his history of the war, in the report of a planning meeting held on 29th May in Algiers, when he was visiting General Eisenhower, who was overall commander in this theatre of the war at that stage. However, just before I was due to set off with the section of the 2nd Lothians involved in the invasion force for this operation on 11th June, right at the last minute I found myself recalled to Algiers.

I was posted to the 26th Armoured Brigade workshops near Philippeville (nowadays known as Skilda) in Algeria, under a wonderful man, Major Desmond Gadsby. I was appointed as Staff Captain (Modifications). At this time the Royal Electrical and Mechanical Engineers (REME) was being formed from the Royal Army Ordnance Corps (RAOC), specialising in the huge task of maintaining and repairing the enormous fleets of tanks and other vehicles being built up, and allowing the latter to concentrate on its more traditional role as implied by the name and relating to guns in particular.

General Tope, from the Royal Army Service Corps (RASC), the section of the Army concerned with the provision and operation of motor transport, had arrived to take charge and the first thing he did – I must say to my complete disgust at the time – was conveyed by his words "I want people in the field at headquarters and I want people at headquarters in the field". What he was aiming at, during a brief spell when there was an opportunity for the building up of better understanding, was that each would have a chance to realise the needs as well as the problems faced by the other. I realised later that he was absolutely right.

I was now in charge of any modifications to tanks, armoured cars or other vehicles, and of course I had learned a great deal from my time as one of those in the field, over the previous five months or so. It was far from easy to keep tanks and their support vehicles in good order when operating in a climate that was hot and subject to sandstorms for much of the year, yet also apt to be muddy in winter in some areas, and over roads that were often poor or non-existent, quite apart from any damage the enemy might inflict. Overheating and far more rapid wear than experienced in Britain were commonplace. It was soon learned that designs which gave satisfactory results at home were often hopelessly inadequate when placed in service in such adverse conditions.

The modifications job was one where my earlier experience, first with buses back in North Western days, and then as a mechanic during my time in the ranks with a Light Aid Detachment, came in handy. For one thing, I knew how the job looked to the man actually doing it and also realised that many of the instructions sent out from England were in terminology he would not readily understand. So I rewrote quite a lot of this material in fitter's language – it was going to be important to ensure that the work would be done properly, wherever it needed to be done. It was also my job to get the parts through and ensure that the work was actually done, so far as practicable.

Even if my job became more desk-bound as Staff Captain (Modifications) from June 1943, it was hardly that of a 'Whitehall warrior'. This was 'The Aufiss', at Phillipeville, actually a Bedford 15-cwt, from which I set about making sure that the tanks and other vehicles in my charge were kept up-to-date. There were many modifications to supervise, often vitally necessary to overcome problems discovered under battle conditions. Apart from the desk and boxes pressed into service as seats, I had some shelves in which I could keep workshop manuals and other paperwork. At least we could roll back the canvas tilt top to keep reasonably cool under the trees which provided shade as well as some degree of cover from air attack, though by then this was less likely as the Germans were pushed back through Sicily and then Italy. Note the nose of one of the big Diamond T tank transporters in the background on the right.

For a time, I was thus a brigade workshops man, increasingly far removed from the scene of battle. In terms of the war, I was less closely involved in events and although my duties were important, they were certainly less dramatic than the first six months in North Africa. Not that my life lacked incident. I went down with malaria in July 1943 and, at the field hospital to which I was sent, met a certain nursing sister called Helen who was to play a big part in the rest of my life – but I'll let her tell that story – see Appendix II.

However, war duties intervened again on 14th March 1944, when the main party of the regiment. 430 strong, disembarked in Naples, the southern part of Italy being by then in Allied hands. My new headquarters was at Caserta Palace, a few miles north of the city. Despite this glamorous-sounding location, I was closer to the down-to-earth world of how to look after vehicles under operating conditions.

A general problem was that though tank crews, and in particular their drivers, were trained for their military duties, they had not always been adequately trained in maintenance. Fortunately this situation had been improved by the better organised systems partly due to the different engineering structure of the army, and partly the adaptation of better routines, as described previously. Another practical point we learned the hard way was to be able to identify fuel, oil and water fillers, sometimes quite similar and close together on a tank, especially in the dark when showing a light might reveal one's position to the enemy.

On a more strategic level, there was a need for more knowledge on how tanks and other vehicles could be expected to behave under widely varying day-to-day conditions. Silly-seeming things would happen, such as vibration causing water drain taps to open, something which could result in a serviceable tank being put out of action, quite apart from a probable wrecked engine to

I suppose I've always been a bit of an extrovert, and so Helen's name simply had to appear on my Jeep. By the time this photograph was taken, the regiment had moved on to Italy, and by good fortune Helen had also been posted there, though even after we were married we could meet only rarely. The little four-wheel-drive Jeep, mud-spattered and lacking its front bumper in this view, was my constant companion, proving a go-anywhere vehicle well-suited to the needs of the time.

This group dates from 1943, soon after I had been transferred to the REME workshops of the 26th Armoured Brigade near Phillipville in Algeria. At the centre of the group is Major Desmond Gadsby, my commanding officer, and I am on the right. Behind is one of the American-built Sherman tanks which were the main type for whose good order I had been responsible during the previous six moinths with the 2nd Lothians.

I was sent to Rimini to take over the field workshop based there and this view of tanks and tranport vehicles parked in the town square was taken in November 1944. By that date, the front line was sufficiently far advanced and allied air superiority sufficient to reduce the risk of enemy attack, making such an assembly of vehicles possible with little risk. As described earlier in this chapter, I had learned the hard way that this was not so when there was a risk of attack by Stuka dive bombers.

change. The heavy steel pins in the tracks of tanks were subjected to heavy wear despite being made of special steel, and if not replaced in time would break, disabling the tank, something that it could be vitally important to avoid in battle, so it became essential to know how many miles they could be expected to cover in varying conditions before this was likely to happen.

One of the simplest modifications with which we were involved by the time the Italian campaign got under way concerned some synthetic rubber hoses on the heavier Churchill tank. They were quite close to an exhaust manifold and the heat from this caused the synthetic rubber to crack, causing a water leak and hence a brewed-up – and quite possibly wrecked – engine. Putting this right did not did not justify referring the matter back to England – so we designed something very simple and straightforward that could be done on

the spot – simply a shield, made of aluminium and asbestos, attached via the manifold nuts, which kept the heat off the hose. The Churchill was relatively new and, in military terms, very important at that time, being Britain's leading venture in the battle-class tank, a category in which the Germans had much strength.

So the modification went out, to be carried out on the tanks in the field. It turned out later that one field workshop had not carried out the work. By that time the Churchills were involved in a major battle that was going on in the north-west of Italy, near the Adriatic coast. Some 70 tanks were put out of action, all 'brewed up' by the side of the road. Such a thing was absolutely criminal, a modern-day near equivalent of the classic story of the battle that was lost for want of a horse that was lost for want of a nail. Inevitably, heads rolled, almost literally – the major in charge was reduced to

Occasionally we had chance to have a look at what the enemy were using against us. Here a captured German Mark IV Special is inspected at Vigrano, as we pressed northwards through Italy.

captain and the captain in charge of the workshop to lieutenant and sent to ENSA, the organisation responsible for organising concert parties for the troops – valuable, but not quite so vital. Ironically, the two demoted officers were subsequently decorated – the recommendations resulting from previous good service were in the pipeline and could not be rescinded.

I was sent to Rimini to take over the field workshop and that was how I came to be promoted to major. Needless to say, I made sure that all modifications were

This was my team, the staff of the REME field workshop to which I was sent on being promoted Major, assembled for a group photograph in the Italian sunshine. We were still wearing the lighter coloured uniforms that had been a feature of the campaign in North Africa, and some variety of headgear is evident, with the beret, generally favoured by the tank regiments to which we were attached, as the majority choice.

Just after the end of hostilities in Italy, two squadrons of the 2nd Lothians changed over to Staghound armoured cars. This view shows one of the 'B' Squadron Staghounds, bound for an occuption role in Carinthia, Austria, passing through Udine – where, coincidentally, Helen's hospital had recently moved. The symbols on the front indicated, from left to right, the regiment, squadron and division to which the armoured car belonged. Note the Bedford 3-tonner following behind – they generally performed well but, lacking four-wheel drive, a towing cable was kept at the ready, draped round the crash bar in front of the radiator.

done immediately. Fate was kind in that Helen had also been sent to Italy, and we were married in Naples on 1st June 1944, though seeing very little of each other as the battles to push the Germans northwards progressed through the winter of 1944-45 – my workshops were based for a time near Forli, on the east coast of Italy.

Eventually, the German armies in Italy surrendered unconditionally on 3rd May 1945. The 2nd Lothians took up an occupation role in Milan and eventually demobilisation led to the Regiment being disbanded in January 1946, but my own release from Army service did not come through until May of that year. Married Sisters had been repatriated first, so Helen had sailed home the previous July, but now we were faced with the new challenges of civilian life.

I seem to have rather a wary expression in this portrait photograph taken as the war ended – it was probably my response to the photographer's instructions, but was perhaps apt, since the future I faced in peacetime had some uncertainties after the clear-cut world of an Army Major.

Chapter Five: Back to buses

With the war over and some important lessons learnt, it was time to take stock. Now there were two of us and I had to think about the future. Clearly my own early experience with North Western and an Army career largely concerned with keeping fleets of fighting vehicles in good order under difficult conditions pointed to a job in civvy street making use of that experience.

The bus industry had changed during my absence. It, too, had to cope with problems – shortages of skilled staff, very few new vehicles during the war years and most of those to the spartan 'utility' specification, the black-out and yet meeting the need to get people to and from the factories that had kept us supplied. Maintenance engineers had performed near-miracles, keeping buses overdue for replacement on the road, but there was much to be done as peace returned. The demand for travel, not only for essential needs, but once again for pleasure, was greater than ever. Private cars were still relatively scarce and beyond the means of most people while petrol for them continued to be rationed for several years. So there was every sign of a job with good prospects.

The organisation of the company side of the industry had changed, too. As I have indicated, in 1942 the rather complicated setup in which many of the companies had shareholdings held by both the BET and Tilling organisations was ended and each group became clear-cut. In practice, each fleet had been managed by one or other of the two groups and most did not alter what had been their main allegiance, but there were some exceptions. One of these was North Western, where the

Tilling influence had been strong, especially in such matters as vehicle policy, for many years. Now it had become a BET company, which was ironic from the Womar family's viewpoint, for as I have explained my father's career had begun with that group.

There was a BET Training Scheme for people regarded as having senior management potential. I applied, and although this may have seemed an obvious step, I did so with some misgivings, for Dad had played a large part in the early development of the bus side of the group's business, and I did not want it to be thought that I only succeeded because of the connection.

The system adopted for the Training Scheme was that most of the four-year period was with one operating company, spending some time in every department, learning something of all the disciplines involved. In my case, it was Maidstone & District Motor Services Ltd, one of the larger companies in the group, covering most of the western part of Kent and not merely the more local area suggested by the title. The fleet strength at that period was about 600 vehicles, split about equally between single and double-deck types, the former including quite a high proportion of coaches, many of which were used on the express services linking London with Hastings and other resorts in the area, though these were only just being resumed in the summer of 1946 after being discontinued during the war.

There were two subsidiary companies, Chatham & District Traction Co, running about 50 double-deckers on former tram routes in that dockyard town, and the Hastings Tramways Co which despite its name had been

After I was demobilised and returned to England, Helen and I took a holiday in the Lake District in the early summer of 1946 before making a fresh start in civilian life. As with almost everything else, cars were scarce and expensive, so we had to settle on this sadly neglected 1938 Vauxhall 10 as our first car.

Maidstone & District claimed that its bus station in Maidstone was the first in the country, having opened in 1922. This scene shows an example of the Bristol K-type chassis with Weymann bodywork, outwardly typical of early post-war additions to the company's fleet, though this particular vehicle was a K6B with Bristol engine, acquired on an experimental basis in 1946. The K6A version with AEC engine remained standard until 1950. The photograph was taken in the early 'fifties, by which date the wartime Daimler of which the rear can be seen in the foreground had received a new Weymann body, and the singledecker, a Bristol L with ECW body, had been added to the fleet.

a purely trolleybus undertaking for many years and also had about 50 vehicles serving what was then quite a busy holiday resort.

Maidstone & District had been under strong BET influence since its early days, and the fleet at that date included a high proportion of Leyland vehicles from the 'thirties, though there had been some AEC batches and, unusually in a BET-managed concern, some Bristol double-deckers. There were wartime utility double-deckers of Bristol, Guy and Daimler makes and for the postwar additions to the fleet it had been decided to standardise on Bristol double-deckers of the K6A type, with AEC engines, and AEC Regal single-deck buses and coaches. Peacetime double-deck bodywork was almost entirely by Weymann while Harrington had bodied the coaches and many of the single-deck buses. The livery in those days was dark green and cream, with a very distinctive style of fleetname lettering.

There were features that were familiar to me from North Western days, such as the Bristol and Leyland chassis, and I had met plenty of AEC engines in my wartime days. But this was almost like another apprenticeship, this time not confined to the engineering

side, though I did find myself crawling under buses – often without pits – and driving them, all over again.

It was an odd life, very lowly in status despite the hope of better things, and not made any easier because of having been through much the same sequence before, managing to climb to a higher plane in my Army days. My pay at that stage was less than a driver received and we didn't find it easy to make ends meet.

Inevitably, one stumbled on things not meant to be seen by a potential member of the management. There was a conductor, for example, who didn't know I was on the training scheme and began to divide the takings of the day's shift, saying "let's see what's ours and what's theirs." On a wider scale, six conductors were caught not collecting fares and promptly sacked, though the Traffic Manager, who happened to be on holiday at the time, reinstated them on his return.

When I joined Maidstone & District in 1946, The General Manager was George Flexman French, who had held the post since 1914 and was the son of Walter Flexman French, effectively the founder of the company. In 1947 he was succeeded by Percy Graefe, who had been the company's Secretary, yet despite this wasn't very good with paperwork. Items piled up in his "in" tray from various departments and outside and nothing much seemed to happen for long periods. It so happened that during the course of my tour round the concern I spent a few weeks in his outer office so as to learn what general managers did.

I suggested that if I prepared heaps of paperwork from his "in" tray so as to divide it into 'extremely urgent', 'very urgent', and 'let them bloody-well wait' (this last a great Army favourite) it might help. He said "Womar, that sounds like a very good idea to me. I'll come in with a pot of coffee and sandwiches over lunchtime and I'll clear as much as I can until we've got it under control".

So I made him a cardboard device with the various categories on it. He came in, as good as gold, the first day complete with coffee and sandwiches, clearing a bit of the 'extremely urgent' and I thought to myself that we were making some progress. However, the next day our Chairman, R. P. Beddow, was due to arrive. Percy took the whole lot – all my gadgets and the piles of paper – chucked them into a cupboard and shut the door. Thus was 'the Womar heap system' quietly forgotten. However, it has to be said that Maidstone & District was a well-run company, continuing to prosper under Percy's tenure of office, which ran until 1954. Smart turn-out of the fleet, both buses and coaches, was a characteristic feature.

So I worked my way round the company. I got to know many people including the senior staff in all the departments. Among those I remember particularly include the Secretary, John Dixon, who was friendly; the Chief Engineer, R. D. Marsall, who was helpful and the Chief Schedules Officer, through whom I obtained modest digs for Helen and myself in Maidstone.

After six months, I was sent up to London to appear before an assessment tribunal to weigh up my suitability as a future General Manager. This was chaired by R. P. Beddow, who was a headquarters Director of BET as well as Chairman of Maidstone & District among several of its subsidiaries. To the left sat Donald Sinclair, General Manager of Midland Red, the group's largest operating company and even at that date a much respected figure, and to the right, Reginald Thomas Ebury, General Manager of the Western Welsh Omnibus Co Ltd. I evidently passed muster, being approved to continue, but I had no idea that about 20 years later I would succeed Sinclair at Midland Red, nor that I would be appointed Deputy Chairman of the Training Scheme.

Not all my training was at M&D, for I spent periods of three weeks each at three other companies to be able to see how methods could vary in response to local circumstances. There were also clear differences in management styles, for in those days BET allowed the local management more flexibility than applied within the Tilling group, where a more centralised system was

The early post-war standard coach in the Maidstone & District fleet was the AEC Regal I with Harrington 32-seat body, the latter built to a style standardised by the company since the mid'thirties. This one, seen parked at Hastings, was new in 1947, having originally entered service in much the same green and cream livery as the buses but seen here in the 'reversed' style adopted for coaches from 1948. The 7.7-litre AEC engine was common to these vehicles and the post-war Bristol K6A double-deckers, of which one is seen alongside.

Maidstone & District had largely favoured Leyland vehicles in prewar days. This Titan TD4 dated from 1935, and was one of a batch of twelve which remained in service through the time I was with the company. They had bodywork built by Short Bros, which had been a major bus bodybuilder as well as aircraft manufacturer until it decided to concentrate on flying-boats after 1936. It was a particularly understandable choice for M&D, being built at Rochester, a town served by the company.

A particularly unusual choice of make was that of Dodge for the chassis of twelve coaches placed in service by Maidstone & District in 1940-41, possibly influenced by war circumstances. This concern, in those days making commercial vehicles of British chassis design but using engines imported from the United States at Kew, Surrey, had an appreciable share of sales among independent operators but this seems to have been the only instance for a major company. Duple supplied the bodywork.

used. So I went off to East Midland Motor Services Ltd at Chesterfield, Ribble Motor Services Ltd at Preston and Western Welsh Omnibus Co Ltd at Cardiff.

Each of these had their own character – and indeed, characters. I met old friends as well as making new ones. At East Midland, Bill Leese, one of my friends from North Western, was Traffic Manager. At Ribble, I met Harry Tennant, later to become Chief Engineer there, and Frank Pointon, later a BET and NBC Director. At Western Welsh, Ebrey's management continued, while at East Midland and Ribble there was a potentially embarrassing situation as my father was a Director of both, but I managed to avoid any difficulty on that account during my brief stay.

By 1949, I was judged fit to be launched into the 'real' world of bus operation.

Chapter Six: Northern battleground

In 1949, I was appointed as Personal Assistant to the General Manager of the Northern General Transport Co Ltd, based at Gateshead, just across the river from Newcastle-upon-Tyne. This had a distinct echo of the beginning of my father's career, for NGT – always known locally simply as "Northern", which was the fleetname displayed on the vehicles, though often called Northern General in industry circles – was a BET company with its origins in one of the group's tramway companies, and only about 30 miles from West Hartlepool, where he had started as a parcels boy with the local BET tramway company in 1908.

Northern General had been formed in 1913 to operate motor buses on behalf of BET in "the Northern Counties", a suitably vague sounding phrase to cover possible expansion, though in particular consolidating the interests in this direction of the Gateshead and District Tramways Co, the Tynemouth and District Electric Traction Co Ltd and the Jarrow & District Electric Traction Co Ltd. It was the Gateshead company that had demonstrated the possibilities, for it had obtained powers to run motor buses in an Act of Parliament mainly concerned with tramway expansion in 1909, and began the operation of buses to Chester-le-Street, about seven miles south along what was then the Great North Road, in May 1913. This proved very successful, some 26 vehicles having been delivered by October and a garage opened in Chester-le-Street, leading to the decision to set up NGT.

The Gateshead company's bus operation was taken over by NGT on 1st January 1914, and on the same day, NGT became the parent company for the three tramway companies – a bold step towards the future, in which the bus would be regarded as dominant, for at the time the three tramways, although modest in scale, were running about 80 trams between them and must have seemed firmly established.

This judgement proved well justified, for NGT expanded quite rapidly, opening garages at Stanley in the western part of County Durham and then, after the 1914-18 war, a new central works at Bensham on the outskirts of Gateshead, which also became the company's headquarters, plus garages in South Shields and Sunderland on the coast, and Consett to the west.

By the time I arrived, the NGT fleet had grown to about 530 vehicles. The Jarrow and Tynemouth trams had long gone, though the Tynemouth company had begun its own bus operation, linked to another local subsidiary, Wakefield's Motors, in due course changing its name to Tynemouth & District Transport Co Ltd. The network of NGT subsidiaries was quite complex, there also being the Sunderland District Omnibus Co Ltd and the Tyneside Tramways and Tramroads Co Ltd, the latter based in Wallsend, both operating buses though again with tramway origins. The Gateshead company was the only one still running trams, having no buses at the time of my arrival, and indeed had become the last BET tramway company to continue with this form of traction, which had been the basis of the group's growth into so many parts of the country.

The combined fleet amounted to over 700 buses, plus Gateshead's 77 trams, and thus the NGT empire had become very substantial, providing the main network of services in much of the northern part of County Durham, as well as to a more limited degree on the northern bank of the river Tyne in what was then the southern part of Northumberland.

The General Manager and Chief Engineer of NGT, and also of most of its subsidiaries, was Gordon W. Hayter. He had held this post since 1936, and before that

When I joined its staff, the Northern General Transport Co Ltd fleet still included quite a number of SOS buses, built by Midland Red, even though the last supplied new to NGT dated from 1934. This IM4 model, No.542 in the fleet, was earlier, having entered service in March 1931, its Short Bros body being to Midland Red's design, as usual with SOS vehicles, although NGT had specified a small roller-blind destination indicator. It was still in largely original condition and remained in service until 1950.

The NGT side-engined buses had chassis designed by Major Hayter and in most cases built in the company's workshops at Queen Street, Bensham, Gateshead, though some of the six-wheelers had been assembled on NGT's behalf by AEC. This is one of the SE4 four-wheelers built in 1938 and having 40-seat bodywork built by English Electric to NGT specification. Donald Sinclair had been Hayter's assistant, becoming Chief Engineer at Midland Red in 1940, and there are hints of his early underfloor-engined buses developed there in the design. No.809 is seen at South Shields, having arrived on the busy main-road service from Newcastle, which could not be operated by double-deckers because of low bridges. Note the air-cleaner, mounted externally above the driver's cab, the aim being to draw clean cool air to the side-mounted AEC diesel engine.

had been Chief Engineer, perhaps being best known for the NGT SE6 and SE4 buses and coaches built for the company's own use in the 'thirties, although they never formed more than a minority of the fleet. He was a remarkable man, with forthright views, often known as Major Hayter – it had been common practice in the inter-war years for former Army, and to a lesser extent, Navy officers to continue to use their rank as a form of title in civilian life. This became less common in the period after 1945, but many of those that had been so addressed in the 'thirties were still known by the names that had become familiar.

As it turned out, NGT found itself in the front line of a fiercely-fought battle of wills, if not of the shooting kind, and I soon found myself involved. What was more, what was essentially the same conflict flared up in the mid 'sixties and once again I found myself in the thick of it, leading an important part of 'the troops'. This was what soon became known as 'anti-nat', in other words anti-nationalisation.

The Labour Government elected in 1945 was committed to a policy of State ownership of key industries, and transport was regarded as one of the most important of these. During the war, the railways had come under close Government control and bus operators were also regarded as forming an essential part of the nation's transport system, as indeed we did. The Labour policy was of an ideological nature, being an expression of the principles laid down in the famous, or infamous, Clause Four of the party's constitution and its reference to 'common ownership of the means of production, distribution and exchange', which is again a matter of controversy for Labour supporters as this volume goes to press half a century later.

The Transport Act 1947 set up the British Transport Commission which, as a first step to the nationalisation of virtually the whole inland transport industry, for which powers were given by the Act, took over the four main-line railway companies and London Transport on 1st January 1948. This in itself gave the BTC a substantial shareholding in most of the major bus companies operating in Britain, for the railway companies had all acquired substantial holdings in the principal companies

operating in their areas around 1929-30. However, it had been agreed with the major bus groups that this would not be such as to give the railways control, and although there was railway representation on the board of directors, management of the companies was left with the groups – generally BET, Tilling, or, in Scotland, the Scottish Motor Traction group.

The Tilling group was strongly influenced by the views, clearly indicated in published statements, of Sir Frederick Heaton, Chairman and Managing Director of Thomas Tilling Ltd, who favoured central control of many aspects of policy and indeed a wider degree of unification of the bus industry as a whole, even if this meant nationalisation. Thus it did not come as a complete surprise when it was announced early in 1948 that sale of the group's bus interests to the BTC was being negotiated – in September, a further announcement stated that agreement had been reached.

The price of BET shares immediately went up in the expectation that the BET board would follow suit, but this completely misread its attitude. The group continued to hold to a fiercely anti-nationalisation line. Mr John Spencer Wills had recently been appointed Managing Director of BET, having expressed the view that it should be fought to the last ditch, a line supported in a statement by BET directors as a whole. It tended to be Spencer Wills who repeatedly made it clear in public utterances that this was the line that BET would follow, rather than the Chairman, R. J. Howey.

Pressure on this matter was intensified during 1949 and it soon became clear that I had arrived in a situation reminiscent in some ways to being sent to the front line in wartime. Early in the year, the SMT group announced that its bus interests had been sold to the BTC, thus leaving BET as the only one of the major national bus company groups to hold out.

In June 1949, the BTC set up a Road Passenger Executive to look after the development of its bus activities. A supreme irony was the appointment of George Cardwell as its Chairman. Readers will recall that he had been my father's boss, both at Hartlepool in 1908-12 until the tramway company there had been sold to the municipality, and then again from 1921 when he sent for him after being appointed to manage the BAT branch at Macclesfield, which later became the North Western Road Car Co Ltd.

The link-up between BET and Tilling had led to North Western being a Tilling-controlled company by virtue of the proportion of shares that company held, and so it was to Tilling headquarters that George Cardwell had been invited in 1930 as a promotion after his period of management of North Western. In 1942 that company was switched to BET control, as I have explained, but Cardwell, was an obvious choice for his new role, with his immense experience. However, an odd situation had been created, for he was on the opposite side to my father, then on the board of several BET companies, including NGT, as well as to me.

What brought the whole situation even closer to me was the proposal that the BTC should set up a series of area boards, expected to be somewhat similar to London Transport in general nature, and the announcement of plans for the first of these, to be called the Northern Passenger Road Transport Board. This had the effect of putting NGT and its subsidiaries under more specific threat of compulsory take-over. The 1947 Act included powers for this, and the proposed area for the Board, while largely based on county boundaries, was such as to take in almost all of the local Tilling subsidiary, United Automobile Services Ltd, which had already become a BTC subsidiary. Its official operating area included the southern and western parts of Durham which NGT did not cover, as well as almost the whole of Northumberland and a slice of north Yorkshire, thus surrounding NGT except on the coastline.

The Northern PRTB was to take over virtually all bus operators in its proposed area – not only all but minor parts of United, the whole of NGT and its subsidiaries, but also seven municipal undertakings and nearly 200 independent operators. The north-east of England has always had many independent operators of

regular bus services – in those days called stage carriage services – some of them in remote rural parts of the counties, but including quite a number of substantial businesses serving mining and other communities. Although the licensing system of those days prevented direct competition, many of them could be regarded as rivals to the bigger companies as the routes they covered were often alternatives in regard to particular journeys.

Outline details of the proposal were published by the BTC in August 1949, and this led to strong local controversy, which did not always follow what might have been expected as the 'party line', this proving enough so to influence the outcome. Although most of the industrial areas surrounding the rivers Tyne (centred on Newcastle, Gateshead, and the string of communities reaching to North and South Shields at its mouth), Wear (centred on Sunderland) and also the Tees (Middlesbrough, Stockton etc, including Hartlepool) very largely voted Labour, there were strong local loyalties.

This applied even within the workforce to some degree, for although the official trade union line supported the nationalisation plans, the local organisations tended to be related to the existing operators' structures, with good day-to-day working relationships. There was a further complication in that many of the company bus men in the area were members of the National Union of Railwaymen, rather than the Transport and General Workers Union, this being partly an after-effect of a brief period when the railways had directly owned some local operating concerns before adopting the policy of taking shareholdings in Tilling or BET-controlled companies.

It was decided that NGT would run a publicity campaign against the proposals, linked to an organisation called the Omnibus Passengers Protection Association (known as OPPA). This had been formed under the active encouragement of one of the BET directors, Peter

NGT operated express services, including that jointly operated with other companies to Leeds, Manchester and Liverpool. Seen here in Leeds in July 1950, with "Private" on the destination blind during a layover, is No.869, one of a batch of ten Leyland Tiger TS8 coaches with Brush 30-seat bodywork dating from 1938 which were regular performers on this duty for many years. The coach livery was cream and maroon. The future of express services was in doubt amid the uncertainties of threatened nationalisation.

York, but found a responsive groundswell among local bus users. Helen had learned to drive a moped by that date and travelled around the local hospitals to recruit nurses, collecting a remarkable number of signatures.

Bus fares in the north-east had remained remarkably low – on company or independent services typical fare values were still 1d per mile, a figure that had remained unchanged since before the war, and this made it possible to draw attention to the 'nationalised' London fares which were appreciably higher. I was given the job of publicising the anti-nationalisation campaign. One of a new batch of Guy Arab double-deckers being supplied to the Tynemouth company was decked out with slogans and posters, carrying the message to the streets. It carried posters for the OPPA, inviting people to join and giving its office address, quite separate from the company, in Jesmond, Newcastle, which was not far from the flat in which Helen and I lived. The poster bus was driven by a driving instructor, A. Tegerdine, who was an enthusiastic supporter. There was some doubt as to whether it would provoke adverse reaction from the drivers and conductors but in fact we had no trouble. I think that the truth was that even though it was an area of strong trade unionism and Labour party support, there was a lack of understanding among the politicians in London of strong local loyalties, giving the OPPA more fertile ground for its campaign than might have been thought – some 100,000 signatures were collected.

In the event, the scheme to set up a Northern Road Passenger Transport Board became bogged down, even if not primarily because of our efforts. They doubtless acted as an irritant to a Government that was having an increasingly difficult time as the after-effects of the war took their toll on the economy. However, the unexpected and more difficult problem was the strong opposition of Labour councillors to the proposal that they should hand over the municipal transport systems to the proposed board. This was another manifestation of local pride and in Newcastle, for example, there was a thriving and well-run fleet of over 500 vehicles, with a programme of tramway replacement by trolleybuses nearing its final stages, as a network of motor bus routes quite a number of services were run jointly with one or other of our subsidiary companies.

Much the same applied on a smaller scale, though without the joint working, at South Shields, where there were municipal buses and trolleybuses and Sunderland where quite a famous municipal tram system was giving way to buses, as well as further south, and outside NGT's area, with municipal undertakings at West Hartlepool (my father's one-time employers), Stockton, Middlesbrough and Darlington as well as a small undertaking run jointly on behalf of two councils on Teesside.

The proposed area scheme proposals were put out for consultation, and the negative response from local authorities was a matter for some concern to the Government, especially as its electoral support could no longer be taken for granted. In the General Election of 1950 the Labour majority was severely cut, leaving the prospect of its continuance uncertain and there was little chance to make significant progress when a further election in 1951 brought the Conservatives back to power at Westminster and the plans for area schemes were dropped.

However, earlier in 1950, when the threat seemed both real and imminent, some County Durham independents had decided to sell out voluntarily to the BTC rather than risk what had seemed almost certain to be compulsory acquisition, with no room for negotiation. This would have created a problem if the businesses in question had simply been added to the United company, infringing the terms of an area agreement with NGT dating back to 1924, so it was decided to create a new company, Durham District Services Ltd on 1st August 1950, to take over Darlington Triumph Services Ltd, Express Motor Services (Durham) Ltd and the ABC Motors consortium. In effect, Durham District acted from its foundation as if it were a United subsidiary, having the same head office but it remained quite distinct, using Tilling green livery, rather than red, until the 'sixties.

Agreements on the boundaries of operating areas had been a feature of company bus operation since quite early in the evolution of the pattern of major companies, it having been felt that it was sensible to come to such arrangements rather than attempt what would have been regarded as wasteful competition between substantial operators, especially where the companies in question had common shareholdings and indeed this had become standard practice in my father's days at the beginnings of North Western.

At the time, the formation of Durham District and indeed the whole company structure of the ex-Tilling companies was doubtless seen as a purely temporary situation, pending the creation of area transport boards. In the event, it and the general status quo, with roughly half the main company fleets in England and Wales owned by the British Transport Commission on behalf of the State, but retaining their company identities and management structure, was to continue until the 'sixties. The area agreements remained, and there were many instances of managers and senior staff in the Tilling and BET companies who had known each other for many years, so the practical job of running the numerous joint services involving concerns from both groups and other activities calling for co-operation continued without difficulty.

Going back to my more general duties as PA to Major Hayter, I soon became friendly with Bob Bailey, who was Assistant Traffic Manager, with an office opposite mine, and indeed his family and mine have remained on close terms ever since, though sadly Bob himself died a few years ago. Our careers were to run in parallel in many ways and we were to meet again at Potteries Motor Traction, as will be recounted later. Before he died, Bob provided some most useful notes, some of which I propose to quote in the text.

Despite my engineering background, my duties with NGT were such that I had only limited contact with the

The 'anti-nationalisation' bus. This was a newly-delivered Guy of the Tynemouth company's fleet, on which slogans and posters filled almost every suitable panel, as well as the windows. Only the 'Shop at Binns' advertisement for a well-known local department store, as found on most NGT group double-deckers, conveyed any other message. The approach, with quite a bit of the flavour of the tabloid press, was centred on the threat of higher fares, and was made easier because bus fares in the north-east generally were among the lowest in the country, and considerably lower than applied in London, so it was possible to make unfavourable comparisons. London Transport, hitherto a 'free-standing' public body, had been taken into State ownership on 1st January 1948, though in fact still run much as before. Just in front of the rear wheel, a poster invites members of the public to join the Omnibus Passengers Protection Association. The bus, T174, was the last of a batch of ten Arab III models supplied in 1949, having the Meadows 10.35-litre engine and bodywork by R. Y. Pickering of Wishaw, a firm with which NGT co-operated in setting up an offshoot called Picktree Coachbuilders at Chester-le-Street. The engines did not prove a success and AEC 7.7-litre engines were substituted.

The NGT SE6 coaches dating back to the mid 'thirties were still being used on touring work, offering exceptional comfort for 28 passengers in two-and-one seating and quiet running with their Hercules six-cylinder petrol engines, even though not always trouble-free in their later years. Seen here in October 1951 outside the George Hotel, Nottingham and looking not out of keeping with what was then the latest trend in coach styling is No.653, one of the first six fo the type, dating from 1935 and with Short Bros bodywork. Some modifications were carried out over the years, notably in 1939 when the original folding roofs were replaced with the style shown, having curved glazing over the cantrails. Note the large hinged entrance door.

fleet, and indeed some of Bob's recollections tend to be more specific than my own in regard to vehicles. At the date I joined, the composition of the fleet was quite mixed. In the late 'twenties and early 'thirties, NGT had been one of the BET companies that had largely standardised on buses built by Midland Red, or to give that firm its full title of those days, the Birmingham & Midland Motor Omnibus Co Ltd, often abbreviated to Midland Red though these older vehicles used SOS as a marque name. Most had gone by the time I arrived, though some of the later ones had been reconditioned, rebodied and fitted with AEC diesel engines, while a few of the petrol examples also survived. A pair of quite remarkable buses had chassis dating back to 1925 though with 1933 bodywork and, because of their normal-control layout, largely used for driver instruction, though still licensed and occasionally used for service – they were probably the oldest buses in any major fleet at the time.

AEC oil engines had also been fitted to many of the NGT SE6 six-wheeled side-engined 44-seat single-deckers built in the mid-'thirties, of which there were about 40, though eight with coach bodywork and some the buses retained the American-made Hercules six-cylinder petrol engines with which they had entered service. Bob Bailey recorded that when he joined NGT in December 1947 some of these were unserviceable as it had proved impossible to obtain spares. An import licence for some replacement engines had been obtained, and these were supplied at a low price, but they proved very troublesome, tending to overheat, causing carburettor trouble and excessive consumption of lubricating oil, particularly on the coaches which had heavier bodywork.

These SE6 coaches were quite luxurious, with seats for two passengers on one side of the gangway, and one on the other, giving a total capacity of only 28 despite their above-average length by the standards of those days of 30ft. When running well, they offered a high standard of comfort, with smooth-running and quiet engines and a very steady ride, but in Bob's view had become unsuitable for continued service, especially on

Perhaps the most amazing survivors in the Northern fleet were a pair of SOS buses of which the chassis dated back to 1925. They had been purchased from Midland Red as charabancs in 1927 but in 1933 the chassis were lengthened and new Short Bros bus bodies fitted, themselves remarkable as they seated 36, possibly the highest seating capacity on a bonneted model of that period. They were retained largely for driver instruction but were still licensed as PSVs and pressed into service when the need arose. Alan Townsin recalls riding from Newcastle to Chester-le-Street in one in 1946/7.

High seating capacity was regarded as important on Northern's single-deckers. Here No. 904, one of the 38-seat AEC Regal buses, is seen in 1946 at Marlborough Crescent bus station in Newcastle, from which the company ran several services to the north-western parts of County Durham, all single-deck. It is bound for Quaking Houses, one of several quaintly named destinations. The vehicle was new in 1939 with the body shown, built by English Electric to NGT specification – it was replaced by a new Picktree body in 1950 and the bus remained in service until 1958.

During the war and afterwards, the use of double-deckers increased in many company fleets because of the numbers of passengers being carried, and Northern was no exception. The wartime Guy Arab, with Gardner 5LW engine, was well received and became the company's standard type in the post-war years. Later examples were 8ft wide and the heavier bodywork gave the five-cylinder 7-litre engine plenty to do, so performance was apt to be limited, but they remained reliable and economical. Here No.1379, an Arab III with Northern Coachbuilders body dating from 1950 – which was just as I was leaving Northern – is seen alongside No.1697, an Arab IV with Park Royal body dating from 1956, in Newcatle in 1958. By that date I had moved on to pastures new a couple of times, as later chapters will show.

the extended tours for which they were used. Even so, they were not withdrawn until 1954, well after I'd left the area completely.

There was a final batch of 40-seat side-engined AEC buses, type SE4, with AEC oil engines from new, dating from 1938, but the bulk of the buses purchased by NGT in the late 'thirties were AEC Regal single-deckers of conventional half-cab layout. There were about 140, and about 90 had been built to a special 38-seat design with unusually short bonnet, to meet Major Hayter's philosophy of favouring maximum seating-capacity single-deckers. There were numerous low bridges, usually carrying railways serving local industries, in parts of the area we covered, notably along the banks of the Tyne between Gateshead and South Shields, for example, making it impossible to operate double-deckers on the busy Newcastle-South Shields service.

This version of the Regal, which the makers described as Regal 'B', had the standard 7.7-litre direct-injection engine, which was a reliable unit – I knew it well from Army days – but to minimise bonnet length, it was

installed close to the radiator, no fan being fitted – there were quite a number of other cases, involving AEC and other engines, where this had been done successfully. The bulkhead was moved forward about 6in, with a cowl over the rear end of the cylinder block, and this made it possible to allow space for an extra pair of seats over the usual maximum for this model of 36.

Bob Bailey told stories of these vehicles being very prone to boiling in hot weather, including one, which had the ring of truth to anyone knowing the area, of a small boy shouting in a broad Geordie accent to the driver in such a case "Hey, Mister, your boiler's bust!" However, the editor of this volume, Alan Townsin, who is a native of Newcastle and remembers many journeys in these vehicles in the period up to 1947, including several on hilly routes in the Consett or Stanley areas, has no recollection of being in or even seeing one that overheated. It seems possible that in their later years, they may have suffered from the effects of the hard water in the area, furring up radiators and engine blocks. It is significant that it was not serious enough to deter many

Like many operators, Northern was short of vehicles in the postwar years and when another BET company, Yorkshire Woollen District, had 25 1936 Leyland Tiger TS7 models surplus to their needs, they were purchased and sent to Picktree for the bodywork, by Roe, to be rebuilt. They entered service in 1949-50, and No.1307 is seen parked at Marlborough Crescent bus station, Newcastle. This was shared with several other operators and a Daimler CVD6 of Venture of Consett, in later years to become part of NBC and ultimately merged with Northern, is visible behind the Leyland. On the right, a Bristol L5G of United can also be seen.

Northern did not buy any new Leyland buses in the early postwar period, and by the time this Titan PD2/3 with Leyland body, N0.1392, entered service in March 1951, I was with the Gateshead company, as described on the opposite page. It was one of a small batch of five, but Newcastle Corporation had a much larger fleet of PD2 models, some of which were allocated to joint services with Gateshead's initial 1950 fleet of Guy Arab buses with 5LW engines, revealing how much difference their more powerful 9.8-litre engines could make when climbing Gateshead's hills. In 1951 we received our own fleet of Leylands, 23 of them 8ft-wide PD2/3 models virtually identical to the bus shown. It is seen at Worswick Street bus station, the other Newcastle terminal for NGT services.

Major Hayter had not given up his unconventional ideas and, in 1951, ten coaches entered service, based on rebuilt and extended pre-war AEC Regal chassis, retaining the 7.7-litre engine, on which were built Picktree 35-seat bodies built to the 30ft by 8ft dimensions by then allowed. Seen here passing through Nottingham on a south-east coast tour in September of that year is 1369, which was based on the mechanical units from 763, a 1937 Regal. The end result was said to be a smooth-running and comfortable coach, though rather heavy for the 7.7-litre engine.

being rebodied, still as 38-seat, in 1949-50 and remaining in service until 1956-58.

There were also smaller numbers of Leyland Tiger TS8 buses and the corresponding Leyland Titan TD5 double-deckers as well as some AEC Regent double-deckers but a major expansion of the double-deck fleet had begun in wartime with several batches of the utility Guy Arab double-decker. These proved reliable and efficient, introducing the company to the merits of the Gardner 5LW engine, long familiar to me from North Western days but not figuring in the NGT fleet until then. It was a bit underpowered for a heavy fully-loaded utility double-decker – Alan recalls an occasion when a driver of one found he had to drop to third gear to maintain speed on a level stretch of road when travelling in the teeth of a gale – the square-rigged lines of the utility bodywork hardly helped in this respect.

Although further batches of Regal and Regent models were delivered in 1946-7, the Regal B was no longer on offer. However, Guy, anxious to keep as much as possible of the market to which it had gained entry due to wartime, proved willing to modify its single-deck post-war Arab model in a similar fashion and Brush built 38-seat bodies to the same general design as that of the 1939-40 Regal on two batches, each of 50 vehicles. Unfortunately the layout of the Guy chassis brought the engine cowl nearer the centre-line of the bulkhead, and it proved necessary to fit the front pair of seats facing rearwards in order to meet the regulations.

More Guy double-deckers were taken into stock and by the time I arrived Guy buses, nearly all with the 5LW engine, formed much of the front-line strength of the fleet. However, a few double-deckers and also some coaches were supplied with the Meadows 6DC engine, which was considerably more powerful, very compact, but unfortunately not so reliable. I was soon to make closer acquaintance with the 5LW-engined Guy in the course of my first appointment to a senior post, as described in the next chapter.

Chapter Seven: Ending Gateshead's trams

As explained in the previous chapter, the Gateshead and District Tramways Co was a subsidiary of the Northern General Transport Co Ltd, but its own history went back much further, to 1880, though operation, at first with steam tramway locomotives and double-deck bogie trailer cars, did not begin until 1883. There were four main routes and three lesser ones. However, in November 1897, the British Electric Traction Co Ltd which itself had been formed the previous year, acquired the company as part of its plan to build up a network of electric tramway systems covering much of the country.

Conversion to electric traction began in 1900 and was completed in May 1901, there having been extension of the existing network in addition to the change of motive power, for which a fleet of 45 new trams was purchased. Further extensions and doubling of track took place by 1904. Gateshead, and Tyneside as a whole, was in a process of expansion of the engineering industry as well as growing in size, thus providing a sound basis for expansion. As it was a statutory company, an Act of Parliament was needed to allow engagement in any new activity. Powers to operate buses and trolleybuses were obtained among the provisions of an Act passed in 1909, although its main purpose as seen at the time was to permit doubling of the track on further tram routes.

The operation of buses began in 1913 and led to the formation of the Northern General Transport Co Ltd, as described in the last chapter. Trolleybus powers were never taken up, though at one stage it seemed as if they might be. The bus business having been hived off to NGT, the Gateshead company remained a tramway operator. Gateshead's position, on the south bank of the river Tyne, directly facing Newcastle on the north bank, made the natural focus for many of its routes the latter city, the largest in the north-east of England, with its capabilities for employment, shopping and leisure. Through working began in 1922, and from then on Gatehead company trams were to be found on many parts of the Newcastle Corporation system, and the latter's trams similarly worked into Gateshead, on jointly agreed timetables.

The original tramway link across the river had been by the High Level Bridge, which was remarkable in that it carried a pair of railway tracks and beneath them, on a separate deck, a roadway with footpaths on either side. Tram tracks were added to the roadway, which had enough headroom and width for double-deck cars, though with little of the latter to spare, a point that was to cause concern in due course, as I will describe later. The company's trams using this bridge mostly terminated in front of Newcastle Central Station, from which main-line railway services to most parts of the country departed.

Tram tracks were also provided on what was called the New Tyne Bridge when it opened to carry the A1 trunk road over the river in 1928. This was a much more spacious construction, from which the design of the Sydney Harbour Bridge was later scaled up. The tram services over it included most of the through routes connecting the suburbs of Newcastle and Gateshead.

The best-known of the Gateshead trams were the long bogie single-deckers seating 48 passengers, of which No. 9 seen here at Central Station, Newcastle, was typical, being one of those built in the 1920s. Most, as in this case, had bodywork built in the company's own workshops. Also visible is one of the six former Oldham Corporation double-deckers acquired in 1947. The trams were always smartly kept; this view dates from 1950, when replacement by buses was already in hand.

From the 'twenties onwards, the Gateshead company tram system continued almost unaltered until the end. Its trams, numbering 77 latterly, included about half that number of long bogie single-deckers, many of which worked along the A1 main road between Gosforth, a suburb to the north of Newcastle, to Low Fell, at the southern extremity of the Gateshead system. Most of these dated from the 'twenties, many having been built in the company's own workshops although there were various cars, mainly double-deck, that had been acquired from other systems.

The double-deckers were single-truck four-wheelers, some having begun life as open-top and although later fitted with top-covers, they remained open ended, although the drivers had been given some protection from the weather with enclosed vestibules. Almost at the end of the story, five more bogie single-deckers were acquired from the Newcastle Corporation fleet, by then rapidly diminishing, and three of these had been rebuilt in 1932/3, making them the most up-to-date cars in the fleet. Yet, all the cars were kept in very smart condition, despite their age.

Newcastle Corporation had begun to replace its trams by trolleybuses in 1935 and this process was sufficiently well advanced by 1939 to cause the subject of similar replacement of the Gateshead fleet to be raised. Gateshead Corporation, which had the right to purchase the system at specified intervals under the powers of the Tramways Act of 1870, but had never exercised it, urged use of the ability to operate trolleybuses that had been held since 1909, but no decision had been taken when the war intervened. The Newcastle conversion programme, largely based on the use of trolleybuses, was resumed when it ended and the Gateshead company drew up one of its own, which would have cost £700,000, a very large sum in those days.

The truth was that, despite its name, the British Electric Traction Co was not enthusiastic about retaining electric motive power in any form. Its once extensive network of electric tramways had gone, almost all having given way to motor buses, and all that was left were the Gateshead system and the Swansea and Mumbles Railway, which although it operated double-deck 'trams' was technically a light railway and not a true tramway. There were two BET trolleybus systems, at Hastings where, as I have mentioned, they were being run by a company which had become a subsidiary of the Maidstone & District company, and at Mexborough & Swinton in Yorkshire, but they were kept on sufferance rather than any enthusiasm and were to be replaced by motor buses in due course.

Another factor was the problem of nationalisation, which made any kind of large-scale investment by a company undertaking based on the expectation of a fair chance of recouping the outlay less attractive, since it seemed unlikely that compensation would be based on such calculations. Indeed, it was the threat of loss of similar investment by the municipalities (Newcastle's large-scale replacement of trams by trolleybuses being a particularly apt parallel) that caused even Labour councils to rebel against the area scheme.

There was quite a bit of manoeuvring by those involved, Gateshead Corporation gave fresh thought to the possibility of purchase of the undertaking, but ran into uncertainties over the running powers in the area of a smaller local authority, Felling Urban District Council. Meanwhile, the company promoted a new Bill, based on conversion to motorbus operation, and after lengthy negotiations an agreement was reached with Newcastle Corporation. There were complex agreements that had been in force since the beginning of joint tramway operation, and recasting these to suit the new situation took time and ingenuity. In the end the services were reorganised to balance the fleets on both sides.

The foregoing was the background to my first senior appointment, which was made in a lavatory during the course of a directors' lunch, incidentally. I was to be

The High Level Bridge across the Tyne was, and is, a remarkable two-level structure, with main-line railway above a roadway which used to carry Gateshead trams – one is seen here emerging on the Newcastle side, passing a Corporation bus awaiting departure from the Castlegarth terminus. The trams were narrower than the buses that succeeded them, and yet did not appear to have all that much room to spare when meeting an oncoming car on the bridge. I found myself with the job of demonstrating that 8ft buses could pass safely on the bridge.

Traffic Manager and Chief Engineer of the Gateshead company, which began to make the initial moves towards the changeover to buses in advance of the event. The Manager continued to be J.W.King, who of course was a tramway man.

An initial fleet of 35 buses was ordered and delivered early in 1950, the choice going to the Guy Arab III with Gardner 5LW engine which was NGT's standard double-decker. The body order was split between Park Royal, Northern Coachbuilders and Brush for speed of delivery. Most of the vehicles were of the 8ft width which was at that time permissible on a route approval basis, rather than the still more usual 7ft 6in. This made them relatively heavy, and the 85bhp 5LW was barely adequate, particularly on the hilly Wrekinton route, a point that was underlined by Newcastle's choice of AEC and Leyland buses with engines capable of developing up to 125bhp for operation on the new joint services. Even so, they were able to provide a much faster service than the trams, and the imbalance was put right on the routes where it proved more of a problem when the balance of the Gateshead company replacement fleet arrived in the form of 37 Leyland PD2 models with similarly powerful engines in 1951.

Training the tram drivers to take over the buses was one of the first tasks, and men used to being near the middle of the road found it difficult to get used to keeping to the left – during training they would sometimes finish up in the middle of traffic islands. In addition, the new buses were much wider than the trams, and this raised particular problems on the High Level Bridge, where the relatively narrow trams did not seem to have all that much width to spare. I had to show, by driving it myself, that an 8ft bus could pass a 7ft 6in one on the bridge, and indeed later that two 8ft buses could pass.

However, all was ready for the first route changeover on 5th March 1950, when the last cross-Tyne tram routes ceased. At that stage the buses were being run by

Bus operation by the Gateshead company began on 5th March 1950, when its official title was still the Gateshead and District Tramways Co, the vehicle shown, No.11, being one of the initial fleet of 8ft-wide Guy Arab III buses with Park Royal bodywork. It is seen on that first rather gloomy day, when the cross-Tyne routes changed from tram to bus operation. The chocolate brown and cream livery gave the fleet a distinctive appearance.

the tramways company, but when the Bill became law on 12th July its name changed to the Gateshead and District Omnibus Company. Further routes changed over to buses in stages during 1951, until the final tram route, to Dunston, was withdrawn on 4th August 1951, thus ending 68 years of tram operation by the company.

More significantly, it brought street tramway operation by the BET group, once the owner of the most extensive chain of tram systems in the country, to an end. To mark this event, the Chairman of BET came to Gateshead to drive the group's last tram, and on some of the photographs taken of that historic event, I am proud to say that I am also visible, standing behind him.

Conversions of the remaining tram routes took place progressively, and this scene marked the end of the Saltwell Park route on 3rd March, 1951. I am present, at the left of the group to the left, looking towards the tram, which was No. 62, one of the last batch of cars bought new by the company, with Brush body on a Brill 21E truck, dating back to 1923. It carried the warning lettering 'Front Exit Car', common to many of the Newcastle fleet, for the benefit of motorists so that they were prepared for passengers alighting from the doorway at the driver's end rather than from the rear platform, used only as an entrance.

Thus the Gateshead company was set on its new course as a bus operator. As it turned out, the ex-tram men made good bus drivers, particularly in the sense that they were used to making frequent stops. They did tend to think that once in top gear that was enough until the next stop, and it was something of a tribute to the flexibility of the Gardner 5LW that, up to a point, they got away with it, as Bob Bailey reminded me in some notes he provided for this book.

We did suffer some brake problems, for the combination of frequent stops and quite hilly terrain, perhaps not helped by the drivers' inexperience, gave them a harder time than applied to the main NGT fleet. On one occasion, I recall having an argument with one of the junior engineering staff who said that the brakes

on a bus which had been the subject of an adverse report were OK. I took the bus, which hadn't been in service long, out on service, only to find that they would barely bring the vehicle to a stop. When we took the drums off, it turned out that the linings on the brake shoes were almost non-existent, and we learnt that much more frequent checking was essential.

The company continued as a separate entity until 31st December, 1975, when it was absorbed by Northern General Transport Co Ltd, with which it had always worked as a close subsidiary. But with the conversion done, my main function was completed in 1951, and I was ready for a call to pastures new.

Above: End of the line. The last Gateshead tram is driven into the depot by Harley Drayton, then Chairman of the British Electric Traction Co Ltd, on 4th August 1951. This was a historic moment, for BET had been set up in 1896 to exploit the possibilities of electric tramways and at one time had subsidiaries operating tram systems in areas in most parts of Britain, and the Gateshead system was its last street tramway. Again, I am present, visible beyond the cap of the inspector in the right foreground. The car was No. 16, one of eighteen bogie single-deckers built in the company's own workshops at the Sunderland Road depot between 1920 and 1928 – like several others it saw further service on the Grimsby and Immingham Railway run by British Railways before being scrapped in 1961. Happily, two such cars were preserved, one being a regular performer at Beamish.

Right: Henceforth, the motor bus took over and the company having become the Gateshead and District Omnibus Company in July 1950 – a limited company of the same name was not incorporated until 1965. In this view, No. 73, one of a pair of Guy Arab buses added to the fleet in 1955 is seen in service. These were of the later Mark IV type and had Metro-Cammell Orion bodywork.

Chapter Eight: Eddison Plant

Working for companies in the BET group had seemed to offer a clear-cut commitment to transport and, in general, bus operation as a line of business – my days at Gateshead had seen the end of the old involvement with street tramways. So when I was asked "Would you like to go to Eddison Plant?", my reaction was almost one of disbelief, for I took the verbal reference to be to Edison, and I began to think of light bulbs, electricity, etc. I protested that I knew nothing about such things, but it was quickly explained to me that this was to a company that had been purchased by BET as part of its decision to diversify into new activities.

There had been considerable BET involvement in electricity generation and distribution, largely as a spin-off from the activity of electric tramway operation conveyed by the British Electric Traction name. The nationalisation of the electricity industry in 1948 had caused the enforced sale of these businesses and released funds to invest in other industries, so BET let it be known that it was interested in purchasing sound companies in the service industries. The uncertainty about the future of the bus industry discouraged further involvement in that line of business, even though BET made it clear that it intended to continue its existing operations and indeed to fight the threat of nationalisation as seen at that time.

So Eddison Plant Ltd was offered, and became a wholly owned subsidiary in February 1949. Its main activity was the hiring out of equipment required for the construction and repair of roads, airfields and associated activities. Although many county councils and other local authorities had large fleets of road rollers, dump trucks and the like, there were wide variations in the need for them, some preferring to hire almost all their needs. When major construction projects were put in hand by engaging contractors, they too often needed large numbers of units for a limited time. By maintaining a fleet of such machines and equipment, distributed among bases in all parts of the British Isles, Eddison Plant could meet much of this need and because of its size, could carry a stock of units which could be moved from place to place as demands varied.

The firm's history was even older than that of BET itself, going back to 1868. An excellent history, called 'A Century of Service' was written for the centenary in 1968 by R. A. Whitehead, the historian of steam road transport and published by Eddison Plant Ltd itself. Space does not allow more than a brief outline here, but the story is an interesting one. The origins were in steam ploughing, and by the 1860s, this was well established. The most successful system used pairs of steam ploughing engines, similar in general form to traction engines, one positioned on each side of a field and each having a large winding drum under the boiler, round which a cable was wound and hauled alternately by one and then the other to draw the plough, itself quite large, to and fro across the field.

Inevitably, the equipment was expensive and only needed briefly on one site, so generally the sets were owned by contractors, who undertook ploughing and

Eddison Plant was a completely unfamiliar part of the world of transport when I joined the firm in 1951 as Chief Engineer. I found myself in charge of a fleet which was largely still in the steam age. Diesel rollers had begun to take over before the war but there were still 290 steam rollers. This is No. 411, an Aveling & Porter machine dating back to 1922, in front of which its driver, Tom House, receives a retirement presentation in the yard at Dorchester, which had been Eddison's headquarters from 1877 until the merger with Banes and the move to Belton, near Grantham – the Dorchester premises were to remain in use until 1965.

related work by the acre. The Eddison family were well established in Leeds, where John Fowler was already established as a maker of ploughing engines at his Hunslet works, and one of the sons became a director of the Fowler company. Another, Frank, bought a pair of engines in 1866 and within a couple of years or so was hiring these out from his farm at Ollerton, Nottinghamshire. Another brother also set up a business in Oxfordshire, but it was Frank who decided to move to Dorset, taking premises in Martinstown, near Dorchester in 1870 and it was from there that the business began to grow. A site in Dorchester itself was leased in 1877, becoming called the Steam Plough Works and remaining in use until 1965. The firm branched into road rolling, as a consequence of the invention of the steam road roller by Aveling and Porter, from the mid-1880s, and this helped to some degree in overcoming the largely seasonal nature of the ploughing business. In those days, the steam traction engine was the only alternative to large teams of horses when heavy loads had to be moved by road, and hence some haulage work was also done.

The development of motor transport brought a need for better roads and wider use of tarmac, so the business grew. By 1904, the fleet had reached over 150, mainly steam rollers and forming the largest available for hire in Britain and, it is thought, the world, at the time, though the area of activity was confined to the south and west of England, generally. There was an agreement between the Oxfordshire company and the main Eddison company giving each spheres of interest (not unlike the agreements that later grew up between bus companies), but there were difficulties as Eddison grew in stature and began to take on work for national road-building contractors, sending rollers and other equipment further to the north and east. Improving techniques helped to make road construction and repair less seasonal, helping to even out demand to some degree.

The 1914-18 war brought a revival to the use of steam ploughs to increase food production, while there was extensive roadbuilding associated with munition factories and ports carrying troops and equipment to France. The fleet of ploughing engines, augmented by specially-commissioned wartime production, and road rollers, were hard at work, especially in 1917-18. Yet with the end of the war, the bottom dropped out of the ploughing business. Farming itself was in a slump and the much smaller and cheaper petrol/paraffin tractor showed itself to be a more economic way of carrying out such work as was needed. Most of the ploughing engines remained unused at Dorchester until sold off in 1934.

The business thus concentrated on road rolling, opening depots at Kingston to cover the area surrounding London and Darlington to serve parts of the north of England, as well as moving into the industrial part of Wales and Scotland. Over 100 new Aveling steam rollers were added to the fleet in 1920-23, largely financed by the makers, but the decline of ploughing and a general slump brought difficulties.

The management passed through different hands with varying fortunes, though Victor Garrett, of the family involved in steam and agricultural equipment manufacture, took over as Managing Director in 1926. The administration was divide into areas, based on the depots at Kingston, Kingsteignton, Brecon, Leicester, Darlington and Glasgow but times remained difficult, with a further threat of bankruptcy, until the mid 'thirties when industrial activity began to pick up, accelerated by the decision to rearm as the threat of war resumed.

Eddison once again found itself involved with defence contracts, and, during the 1939-45 war, was again working flat-out. Finding drivers who could run and maintain steam rollers was almost impossible, and one story of an 82-year-old, Bill Saunders, still working seven days a week and ten to fourteen hours a day to complete an urgently needed Fleet Air Arm base near the Lizard illustrates the point. Some 323 airfields and about as many other military installations were rolled by Eddison, an impressive record for a firm that had been at death's door fifteen years earlier.

A steam fleet

However, the fleet was still largely steam, with an age between 24 and over 50 years and the cost of the wholesale replacement by diesel rollers was beyond the company's capabilities without fresh capital. Banes and Co Ltd was an up and coming concern, itself having origins in an old-established roller-hire business of Frank Banes at Potton, Bedfordshire, but taken over in 1942 by a new company of which Mr Edward Barford of Aveling-Barford Ltd and some associates were leading shareholders. In addition to a fleet of modern Aveling diesel rollers there were a growing number of dumpers of the same make. Negotiations for a take-over of Eddison Steam Rolling Co Ltd by Banes led to agreement in 1946, and although the former at first continued at Dorchester, the headquarters were moved to Syston Lane, Belton, near Grantham and full merger was followed by Banes & Co Ltd being renamed Eddison Plant Ltd early in 1948.

A further stage in the reconstruction led to the sale to BET the following year. Raymond Birch was a member of BET's directorial staff and chairman or a director of a number of bus companies in the group. His family's firm, Birch Bros Ltd, established in 1832, had run buses in London in pre-London Transport days, and still ran services to Bedfordshire, though this business remained independent. He had negotiated the Eddison purchase for BET and, becoming Chairman, realised the need for changes in methods as well as equipment. To implement this, he had the expertise of John Spriggs, trained as an engineer and coming to the firm via the Aveling-Barford connection, who was appointed Joint Manager – it was with him that I was to work particularly closely. At that time the firm had a fleet of some 290 steam rollers, 182 heavy diesel rollers, 71 light rollers, 38 dumpers and 13 other major items. Thus there was still a considerable way to go in replacing the steam roller fleet, and although far from young in years, enough of these were still sound enough not to demand over-hasty replacement.

There was still a seasonal variation in demand for road rolling work, partly related to weather and partly to local authorities tending to run out of funds for major projects at the end of the financial year ending in March, and it was decided to look for items which would be in more regular demand. These tended to be more associated with general constructional work rather than road building, including items such as compressors, and the firm also expanded by acquiring companies already hiring such equipment.

I went for interview in April or May 1951, having been told that the objective was to introduce bus fleet engineering methods. I was offered the job and was told that I was to have something ready for the managers' meeting to be held in October, attended by people from all the local depots in England, Scotland, Wales and Ireland (where a branch had been established in Dublin in 1947). I had to go round and inspect all the 1,400 items of equipment of one kind and another, whether in use or broken down. The latter was not uncommon, and in Ireland I found a case where 'Steam Roller Corner' was the name given to a location where a broken-down roller had become part of the landscape, to the extent that grass was growing right through the roof!

As I travelled round, I got to know more about the people involved, and many of the older men that had driven steam rollers for much of their lives were real characters. Their homes were the living vans that they towed around behind their machines. Sturdily built to withstand the effects of travel on iron-tyred wheels, they were often very dirty within, though the steam rollers themselves were maintained with great pride, and inside the vans there was often a picture of the Queen. Most of the men lived a lonely life and it was standard practice when one died to look under the mattress in the van, for there would often be several hundreds of pounds (a great deal of money in those days) that they had put away from their pay. They could live very cheaply, and there was little to spend their money on. It was a job that tended to appeal to the kind of person that did not mind being constantly on the move. A few were married, their wives living with them in the vans, but this was less common.

Eventually, I got round to see all this stuff, helped by all the local managers, such as Paddy Donnelly in Dublin, who was a former fighter pilot and a great character. I made an assessment of what it was going to cost to put it right, which shook everyone a bit, and set up an appropriate overhaul and modification system. In addition to my knowledge of bus company methods, I was able to draw on Army experience, which was quite useful, for many of the depots had been set up when funds were low and they had limited facilities, so a knowledge of how to keep tanks in good order in the field of battle helped to arrive at a system that would work in places without elaborate workshops.

I had the benefit of access to the work being done on improved maintenance methods within BET, the commercial vehicle industry generally and associated

The steam roller drivers were individualists, prepared to lead what could be a lonely life, constantly on the move. Tom House is seen at the controls of No. 411, the 1922 Aveling & Porter shown on page 43.

There was pride in the turn-out even of so venerable a machine, and the inevitable smuts were wiped away daily.

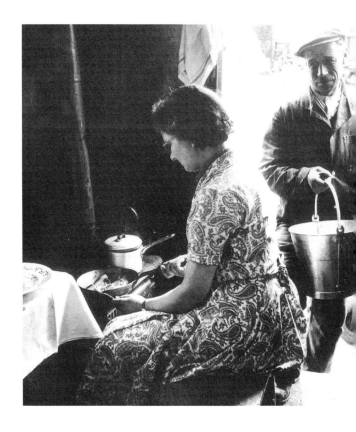

Tom House was one of the minority of steam roller drivers who were married. Here, there is an appreciative-looking smile as his wife cooks bacon for breakfast in the living van – note the white tablecloth.

organisations, such as the development of detergent lubricating oils, then being adopted for diesel engines and which had shown good results in bus fleets. Such lubricants offered strong advantages in the construction industry, with its arduous working conditions, and the whole question of maintenance methods had to be rethought, as the circumstances were quite different to those in the bus industry. For one thing, the fleet was dispersed all over the country and frequently away from its nominal operating bases for long periods, wherever the work took the rollers and other items. They were being used by the hirers and inevitably, the relationship was quite different to that in the bus industry, where the vehicles were owned and operated locally by one concern, itself often a member of a well-organised group with its own specialised purchasing organisation, as operated by BET.

The new diesel rollers we were buying at the time I joined the firm were of various makers' standard types. Among them were Aveling-Barford, Green, Marshall and Wallis & Stevens, although there were also a few German Zettelmeyer machines for use in Eire. My survey of the fleet and its needs reinforced the view already being formed in particular by John Spriggs that none of the types available were well suited to our needs. The prewar Aveling diesels had been simple and robust, but post-war rollers were more complicated, with poor access for maintenance and not sufficiently flexible in their capabilities for the company's needs. All had conventional clutch and gearbox transmission, and although this was simple in principle, it was not well

suited to rolling work, with its frequent reversals of direction.

Ford was by this time making a four-cylinder diesel engine developing 50 bhp at 1,800 rpm, which was about right for our needs, but the real breakthrough was the discovery that Brockhouse had made a prototype torque converter matched to this engine. At that stage, the use of automatic forms of transmission for this type of machine was quite rare, but it held particular advantages for road rolling, where there were the frequent changes of direction and a need for smooth take-up of the drive to produce a level surface. Eliminating the jerk

Eddison depots were sited to serve the spread of demand for equipment over the country. This scene, at Maidstone in the early 'sixties, dates from a little after my time with the company, and shows a grader being driven on to a low-loading trailer hauled by a Bedford TK tractive unit allocated to the depot.

as the drive was apt to be rather abruptly re-engaged after reversing direction proved to be an important advantage that came to light when machines of this type began to enter regular service.

In 1955, having got the approval of the board, we began a series of experiments with the aim of arriving at a satisfactory design. The Belton works were not large and the firm had not attempted the design and construction of a prototype before the work began. The aim was simplicity, and although we began with sketches of what we were proposing, much of the 'designing' of the larger items was done with chalk on the workshop floor!

Inevitably, with a small team, limited facilities and the work of improving the maintenance arrangements for the fleet also still in hand, work was slow, and we were keen to make sure, sometimes by trial and error, that each part of the design was 'right' before going ahead. There was some initial testing to be done, though the machine performed just as we had hoped and proved encouragingly trouble-free, so it was not until 29th March 1957 that the prototype was ready to be shown to the trade and the trade press. At that point, the new roller was given the name Eddimatic Torque Ranger in place of its simple development code ER.

Trials in service led to confirmation of the decision to go ahead with plans to find a manufacturer willing to build the machine in quantity. Thomas Green & Son Ltd of Leeds was chosen and the formal order for an initial run of eight production rollers was placed in May 1957 for delivery by the end of the year, followed by 20 more by the end of March 1959. Ultimately, 250 were built, and they proved very successful – I think we may have helped to convince the road construction industry of the advantages of torque converter transmission for such work.

In 1958, I returned to the bus industry, as will be described in the next chapter, and my career did not take me back into the road construction or plant hire business, but a few years ago I went back to Belton to see how things had developed. The Eddimatic machines had proved very successful, and even the prototype had given good service despite its 'knife and fork' methods of construction. It was a good demonstration of how careful assessment of needs and sound engineering principles – not least the determination to keep things simple wherever possible – will produce an effective result. It had been an instructive period of my life, but I was glad to be getting back to buses.

The original Eddimatic prototype seen (above left) before the cab was added. When it was first completed and before it was licensed, we took it out on the road from the Eddison works at Belton to see how it behaved, completely forgetting about trade plates and insurance, and were engrossed in its promising behaviour. In due course a police car appeared, its occupants taking an obvious interest in the proceedings but, fortunately for us, no action. We scuttled back as soon as they had gone. The same machine, completed and christened the Eddimatic Torque Ranger, is seen (above right).

The Eddimatic was developed into a pneumatic tyred form, the rows of wheels arranged to give complete coverage of the surface as the second rolled over the gaps left by the first.

Chapter Nine: Potteries Motor Traction

In the summer of 1958, I achieved what had been my ambition since boyhood, to become the Chief Engineer of a bus company. The concern in question was the Potteries Motor Traction Co Ltd, based at Stoke-on-Trent. Its history was similar to that of Northern General Transport in having been a tramway company, though its origins were even older, going back to 1861, when the tramway pioneer, George Francis Train, dug the first shovelful of earth for a line from Bursley to Hanley. That and other routes were operated by horse-drawn trams, and these were followed by steam-hauled cars from 1881, though these proved controversial on the grounds that they were dirty – doubtless because of the smoke – and the roads too narrow for such 'offensive' vehicles and for a time they were withdrawn.

The solution came with the acquisition of the system by the British Electric Traction Co Ltd, the undertaking being one of its first purchases. The business was given the title Potteries Electric Traction Co and electric trams began operation in 1899. The network linked the 'five towns' – Stoke-on-Trent, Newcastle-under-Lyme, Burslem, Hanley and Fenton (the last-mentioned in more recent years overshadowed by the growth of its neighbour, Longton) – which together comprise the district known by the name of its main business and made familiar to many by Arnold Bennett's novels, in which the tramways are mentioned frequently. The system ran quite successfully until the 'twenties by which date competition from independent motor bus operators was becoming severe. The PET company itself had experimented with motor buses as early as 1900, but it was not until 1913 – the same year as with NGT – that buses began to be operated successfully, at first on a small scale with four Daimler CD-type single-

deckers, but gradually growing, with routes extending beyond and between the tram routes.

In 1926 the then bold step of replacing the trams by buses began, and the system, which had run about 120 trams at its peak, gave way to buses completely by 1928. The new buses, at that stage all single-deck, were SOS models, made by the Midland Red concern, and this make was still standard when the company's title was rather belatedly changed to Potteries Motor Traction Co Ltd in 1933, and that title remained right through to the end of the NBC era, though the initials PMT began to be used as the fleetname in the post-war period. Double-deckers had begun to enter the company's service in the early 'thirties and their proportion steadily increased on the urban routes where they could be used, though services had extended well beyond the 'five towns' area, and in the north the company's territory extended to meet familiar ground to me where North Western held sway. To the south, our 'neighbour' was Midland Red, BET's largest subsidiary and later to play a key part in my story. PMT began to buy Leyland vehicles in 1933 and the company was unusual among BET fleets in also favouring Daimler in the late 'thirties.

There were still many independent operators in the area at that time, some of them quite large, but gradually the businesses and vehicles of these were acquired, tending to make the content of the fleet unusually mixed for a major company. This process continued during and after the war right up to the time when I joined the company, and in addition new purchases included AEC, Daimler, Guy and Leyland models of quite a variety of types.

A summary of the fleet make-up dating from a few months before I arrived quoted 205 double-deckers, 249

The PMT fleet was very mixed but the standard modern single-decker when I arrived was the AEC Reliance with Weymann 44-seat body, this latter being to the BET Federation specification, as widely used in the group at the time. The vehicle shown was one of the batch of 40 dating from 1955, SN5581, seen in Derby, but ten dating from 1954 plus further additions in 1956 and 1957 brought the total of similar buses to 86 at the time I arrived. They were generally well-liked, apart from the tendency to cylinder head gasket failure typical of the type.

Leyland chassis had been quite strongly represented in earlier post-war purchases. This Leyland Tiger PS2/5, No.434, was one of 14 with Brush bodywork to Federation specification dating from 1950. It is seen in Buxton, where PMT buses ran into North Western territory very familiar to me. Such buses, seating only 34 yet requiring a crew of two, were becoming uneconomic to operate – the batch was withdrawn in 1962.

A large intake of second-hand vehicles had been made in 1951, when five independent operators were acquired, though some ran as subsidiaries until 1952. This Guy Arab III single-decker with Duple 35-seat coach body, which PMT numbered as SN334, had been one of 30 vehicles operated by Stoke-on-Trent Motors Ltd.

PMT had been among a minority of BET companies in favouring Daimler buses in the 'thirties and, to the extent of one batch, 'forties but this single example, H500 in the fleet, earned its place in history by having the first MCW Orion lightweight body, built in this case by Metro-Cammell, and exhibited at the 1952 Commercial Motor Show. The chassis was of type CLG5, a short-lived Daimler variant intended to exploit the strong interest in weight-saving at that time – as completed, the bus weighed only 6tons 2cwt, about 1½tons less than most double-deckers of the period. PMT took only the one example, though 30 CVG5 with the same Gardner 5LW engine were added to the fleet in 1956, half with a production version of similar bodywork.

single-deckers and 52 coaches on chassis which comprised 233 Leyland, 184 AEC, 71 Guy, 60 Daimler, five Commer, three Crossley, one Maudslay and one Morris-Commercial. Bodywork showed even more variety, being listed as 37 Brush, four Barnard, sixteen Beadle, 54 Burlingham, three Crossley, seven Duple, nine Lawton (this being a local concern), five Leyland, 37 MCW, seven Massey, four Metalcraft, 148 Northern Counties, four Park Royal, nine Roe, two Strachans, 145 Weymann, five Willowbrook and ten Windover. Hardly a standardised fleet! Yet even this did not convey the variety, for the Leylands, AECs and Daimlers included

Guy Arab double-deckers with Newcastle on the destination blind and Gardner 5LW engines under the bonnet had echoes of my days with Northern, but this scene was in Newcastle-under-Lyne. The Arab IV nearer the camera was H538, with Weymann-built Orion body, new in 1953. On the left is L242, a wartime Arab II with Stachans utility body. We used the H or L prefix letters to help in distinguishing highbridge and lowbridge bodywork, a matter of some concern as there were low bridges affecting several important routes. The white steering wheel was also used to draw attention to the vehicle's height, yet from time to time vehicles would be taken down the wrong route, quite often with quite serious damage as a result.

quite a range of different types, and the ex-independent vehicles in particular included a bewildering collection of body type variations.

So I had plenty to do in ensuring that this lot were kept in good order, and my initial impression was that the fleet looked a bit dowdy. In fairness, it was a difficult area for vehicles to work in, with a fair amount of industrial pollution in those days. Operating conditions were quite tough, with numerous stops on the services running in and between the five towns.

There was also a problem with low bridges, there being three, including one in the centre of Stoke, too low for double-deckers of any kind, as well as others which would not permit the use of highbridge (full-height) types. Accordingly, a high proportion of the double-deckers were of the lowbridge type, which at the time I joined the company were of the traditional style with sunken side gangway on the upper deck and very inconvenient for both the passengers and the conductor. There were some of the conventional centre-gangway highbridge type and inevitably, every year without fail, one or possibly two vehicles would stray off the intended route and slice the roof off. It was a miracle that no-one was killed. The basic problem was that the driver was not conscious of the upper deck above him and to reinforce the warning notices, I came to the conclusion that we should try using white steering wheels on double-deckers – in the end I think there were ten different ways of reminding drivers of the problem, yet I have to admit that when I left the company we were still suffering about the same rate of this type of collision.

Yet there is more to the Chief Engineer's job than looking after the fleet. There is the responsibility for the premises, and in particular the garages, and the relationships with the other members of the firm's personnel, and indeed with everyone from the Chairman down to the most junior of one's own staff. In day to day terms, I was responsible to the General Manager. When I arrived, this was Warwick Wroth, whom I knew from North Western days and with whom my relationship was a little awkward. However, within a few months S. J. B. Skyrme was appointed to succeed him, and matters improved.

Of course none of us then knew that Jim Skyrme would rise to become Chief Executive of the National Bus Company, or indeed that there would be such a concern. He had risen through a succession of jobs within the group, and at one time had been Chief Engineer of North Western. It was common practice for engineers to compare notes on their problems with their opposite numbers in associated companies. It was understandable for, if the same difficulty had been experienced and overcome, a lot of time and trouble could be saved. So one day Jim rang Harry Tennant, Chief Engineer at Ribble and in those days senior to him, about some problem, and perhaps had repeated the process a little too often or it had been a bad day for Harry, but he was told "I'm fed up with you, Jim, ringing me – go and sort your own problems out!"

A little later, though before he came to PMT, Jim Skyrme had become General Manager with East Midland Motor Services, and his Chairman at the time was my Dad. They were looking around a garage and Jim raised the question of garage heating, saying it was very expensive and suggested that the heating system be relocated in the roof instead of at a lower level. Dad said "All you're going to do is warm sparrows' behinds (only he didn't say quite that), Skyrme". So they then went to the Board meeting, at which the subject was on the agenda, and Skyrme sat there quietly, expecting to be shot down in flames. Dad said, "Mr Skyrme has come up with a very good idea, and I think it is high time we started heating from the top of the garage instead of the bottom". In fact, heating systems mounted quite high on garage pillars but directing heated air downwards became quite common, helping to simplify the necessary plumbing.

A detail garage problem that I had to tackle at PMT

PMT also operated coaches, this Leyland Royal Tiger with Burlingham Seagull body being one of ten dating from 1952. It was numbered C519 in the fleet, and is seen visiting Colwick race course, Nottingham.

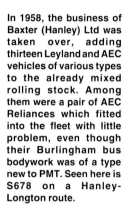

In 1958, the business of Baxter (Hanley) Ltd was taken over, adding thirteen Leyland and AEC vehicles of various types to the already mixed rolling stock. Among them were a pair of AEC Reliances which fitted into the fleet with little problem, even though their Burlingham bus bodywork was of a type new to PMT. Seen here is S678 on a Hanley-Longton route.

was an excessive number of accidents within garages, usually caused when buses were being reversed, hitting pillars or the wall. It had been the practice to paint such surfaces in dark colours on the basis that exhaust smoke tended to blacken them. However, this was causing drivers not to see them. So I introduced a colour scheme of quite a light shade of blue and white. A dramatic drop in such accidents resulted and while I was there all the depots were treated similarly. Another aspect of this was the brighter look it gave – it had struck me that it was bad psychology to expect men and women to come in at ungodly hours of the morning and all kinds of weather to work in places that looked like dungeons. So it worked out quite well.

Not long after Jim Skyrme had arrived at Potteries, we went to visit the Gardner concern at Patricroft, near Manchester, to discuss engine matters with the great Hugh Gardner himself. On the way back he said "Walter, we are going to the Cat & Fiddle to have a nice meal", this being a well-known pub at the summit, 1,690ft, of the climb on the Buxton-Macclesfield road, and the terminus of one of North Western's toughest routes, incidentally. The weather was foggy and cold, but even so, his car, a Wolseley, began to pink and boil. He was

driving and had arranged to meet a pal of his, so eventually we staggered up to this place. As he got out of the car, he said "Now, Walter, you sort the car out" – I, as his Chief Engineer, thus being put on my mettle.

So there I was, standing in the perishing cold – I don't think I even had a jacket on, trying to find out what was causing the trouble, when along came a young lad. He said "Are you having trouble with the car?" I said "Yes" and he said "I'll have a look at it". He couldn't have been more than fifteen, and he proceeded to poke about with his fingers and after a while found that a core plug had failed behind the exhaust manifold, which was still very hot. I couldn't have stood putting my hand there, no way. "Oh, Crikey", I said, "there's half-a-crown, good lad, off you go". So I went into the pub and said to Jim "I've sorted it out; you've got a core plug gone". He asked where it was, so I said "Behind the red-hot exhaust". Years later, I heard that he told people "That's when I knew Walter was an engineer!" Little did he know the true story.

However, I was fortunate in having a good friend within the company, for the Traffic Manager was none other than Bob Bailey, my colleague from NGT days, who had arrived there before me. Sometimes the

At first glance, the Albion Aberdonian with Weymann 44-seat body looked much the same as the similarly-bodied AEC Reliance or Leyland Tiger Cub, the fleet also including 20 of the latter. But the Aberdonian carried the concept of lightweight construction a little too far, certainly for PMT's tough operating conditions. A clue was given by the lighter-looking eight-stud wheels and hubs, for the brake assemblies within them proved unable to stand up to hard driving, with frequent stops on hilly routes. Here SN8737 of the 1958 batch is seen at Derby on the 23 service, working to Uttoxeter on a wet July day of that year.

relationship between the traffic and engineering departments can be a little difficult, for the priorities of the two are fundamentally different. Basically the traffic man wants the whole fleet always to be available and is apt to forget that buses need maintenance and overhaul, and that this means that they have to be off the road from time to time, quite apart from situations when they unexpectedly give trouble.

Usually, new buses improve reliability and are expected to able to be able to do the work for which they were purchased with no more than servicing for a reasonable period of time. Sadly, this was not the case with some new additions to the fleet which added yet another make just after the analysis I quoted earlier in this chapter had been carried out, shortly before I arrived. This was Albion, though no doubt the initial four examples of the recently introduced Aberdonian lightweight single-deck model delivered in the latter part of 1957 had been chosen partly on the basis that they used the Leyland O.350 engine, a type which was giving good service in a batch of Tiger Cub models already in the fleet. There had been various second-hand Albions taken over with independent operators' fleets, but these had been sold off before my arrival, not so far as I know because of any particular problems but to keep the maintenance complexities of coping with non-standard types within reasonable bounds.

Albion had been taken over by Leyland in 1951, and subsequent models were intended to fit into gaps in the latter's range. A small lightweight model in what would nowadays be called the midibus class called the Nimbus had been introduced, using a four cylinder version of basically the same engine. The Aberdonian was, in effect, an extended version of much the same design, but with the O.350 5.76-litre six-cylinder unit. The Tiger Cub had been regarded as a lightweight model, taking up to 2 tons off the weight of the original Leyland underfloor-engined model, the Royal Tiger.

The Aberdonian took weight-saving even further, slicing another half ton or so off the Tiger Cub's weight and hence doubtless seemed to give the prospect of even better savings in running costs, very much in mind at the

time under the pressure of increases in wage costs and the beginnings of falling revenue, as private motoring began to expand. It also had the benefit of Albion's five-speed gearbox, which proved to suit the O.350 well. Yet overall, it was perhaps a case of a 'slice too far', for the chassis design, and particularly the brakes, were not really up to the tough conditions imposed by the frequent stops and heavy use on intensive bus duties, especially in quite a hilly area. Unfortunately for us, 30 more had been ordered, arriving in 1958, and at first were put to work in the hilly Milton area, but after quite a short period they simply had to be taken off such duties and moved to areas such as Stafford and Market Drayton, where there are few hills and services were less tightly scheduled.

A different kind of challenge, but again bringing trouble with a new model, was represented by the Leyland Atlantean in its original production PDR1/1 form. From a traffic point of view, it seemed to be just what PMT needed for its intensive routes. The 1956 prototype had visited the company and offered a combination of high seating capacity with low-floor layout and hence the use of centre gangways on both decks with 'lowbridge' overall height. Such was the confidence in the model that the initial order was for 35, delivered in 1959. These was also low height vehicles, but the design had been altered so as to allow use of a more conventional rear axle, and thus these buses had what amounted to the traditional lowbridge layout at the rear of the upper deck.

However, I soon found myself more involved in coping with more practical problems in keeping them running. The early Atlantean soon became quite notorious for its mechanical failures, and it was evident that Leyland had not spent enough time confirming its reliability after what was quite an extensive redesign from the prototype. This was the first rear-engined model to go into large scale service with a variety of operators in Britain and everyone involved had a lot to learn.

One of the problems was due to the remoteness of the engine and gearbox from the driver. Partly because of

A dramatic change in double-deck bus design was afoot, and as often so in such circumstances, it was not without its headaches. In 1957, PMT's final batch of new front-engined double-deckers had entered service, in the form of fifteen Leyland Titan PD3/4 models with synchromesh gearboxes and Metro-Cammell front-entrance bodywork. The seating capacity was 68, which was as high as could be negotiated with the trade union, which always tended to be 'difficult'. By that date, the PD3, basically a PD2 extended to the 30ft length which had become permissible for two-axle double-deckers from 1956, was a well developed and reliable model – these examples ran with very little trouble until 1971-72. Seen here in Newcastle-under-Lyne is H712.

The Leyland Atlantean gave the promise of a solution to several problems, not least for PMT that of a high-capacity double-decker with low overall height. Some 90 entered service with PMT in 1959-61. but keeping them running proved something of a nightmare, with transmission failures and overheating as regular problems. They all had Weymann low-height bodywork, seating 73 or, in the final batch, 72 – seen here is L869 of that series, bound for Silverdale on the 103 service from Longton.

this, semi-automatic transmission was adopted, with electro-pneumatic control for the epicyclic gearbox. The driver had a small gear control lever mounted on the steering column, and it was all too easy for him to flick this into positions which put almost impossible demands on the units nearly 30ft behind him, not receiving anything like the same sense of what was going on when the engine was alongside him in the cab. Although similar epicyclic gearboxes had proved reliable in front- or mid-engined vehicles, failures began to be quite frequent, and Leyland also introduced another problem with an attempt to combine the fluid flywheel and friction clutch, the latter intended to lock up and give a solid drive at higher engine revs. In practice the mechanical clutch mechanism wore, causing an excessive amount of clatter and didn't engage smoothly.

There was also a tendency to overheat, and for a time this was apt to be a problem with rear-engined models generally. Part of the cause lay in the concentration of mechanical units behind the rear axle, in an area which received no natural cooling flow of air as applied at the front of the vehicle and was itself apt to pick up heat from the rear brakes on stopping service. In addition, the provision of heaters within the bodywork provided numerous sources of minor leaks, the problem often being of air getting into the system and causing air locks. Still, we persevered, and indeed more Atlanteans were bought, 40 in 1960 and fifteen in 1961, all with the same type of low-height body, since they suited PMT's needs so well from a traffic department viewpoint.

For single-deck additions to the fleet, we reverted to the AEC Reliance underfloor-engined model which had been the usual choice since 1955, apart from the Aberdonian episode, and which included both bus and coach versions. The former mostly 44-seat of the usual BET style of the period either by Weymann or Willowbrook. They gave good performance but the wet-liner AH470 engine was very prone to head gasket trouble, especially if driven fairly hard, as was unavoidable on many of our services. Even so, this was a drawback we could live with, for in other respects they were generally trouble-free and quite popular with the staff.

The process of take-overs of independent operators was still proceeding, and the take-over of W. S. Rowbotham of Harriseahead in 1959 brought yet more variety to the fleet. Some vehicles were sold off quite quickly, but a vehicle that was kept and ran for about 5 years with PMT was a Foden double-decker dating from 1952. It had a Gardner engine, which was both familiar and known to be reliable, though it was a 6LW and most of those in Guy Arab and Daimler buses in the fleet at that time were 5LW units, but the general chassis design was quite straightforward and thus the extra make did not create much of a problem. Other acquisitions kept in the fleet for some time included one of the rare Dennis Lancet UF underfloor-engined models, with Plaxton coach body.

This background of large-scale independent operation in the area and the gradual process of take-over of these fleets by PMT had a bearing on one of our biggest problems. The independents generally did not recognise trade unions and the latter's strength within PMT was patchy. It is easy to forget just how powerful the trade unions were in those days, even though there was a Conservative Government at the time, and what was more, the unions wanted PMT to become a closed shop, in which all employees would be required as a condition of employment to be union members. This, in turn, meant that the unions would have a stranglehold on the firm and hence we, as the management wanted to prevent any such thing.

The problem was all the greater because quite a large section of the industry, either State-owned as a consequence of the actions of the earlier Labour Government or municipal undertakings, particularly where there were Labour councils, did work on the closed shop principle, whereas BET, still very much a private-enterprise concern, was against it in principle as well as practice. My time as Chief Engineer brought me into frequent contact with this problem, for it applied to the workshop staff as well as the road staff.

Another facet to the political climate in which we operated was the way in which PMT was almost like a municipal undertaking itself, in the sense that it served mainly the five towns built-up area. There were very few large industrial cities or towns that did not have a municipal fleet in those days, but this was one of them. As was rather to be expected in an area of this type, for the Potteries name was an apt one, and most of the nation's crockery came from its factories, the Stoke-on-Trent Council was Labour-controlled, yet a good relationship existed between them and PMT – it could almost be said that we had the advantages of a Corporation undertaking without the disadvantages. As was so often the case, local personalities often had a will to overcome problems which transcended political views, and some of these people were colourful characters with whom it was not difficult to work once a clear understanding of the objectives was established.

I become General Manager

As it turned out, I found myself with much broader responsibility for such matters, as part of those in running the whole company, when appointed General Manager of PMT with effect from 1st January 1962. It was by no means common for a Chief Engineer to be promoted in this way, and quite commonly the pathway upwards was to be moved to a smaller company for the first managership. Jim Skyrme had been moved on to take over the General Manager's role at Southdown. I have to confess that I took a certain delight in winning the Coach of the Year award at the British Coach Rally in Brighton with one of a new batch of AEC Reliance 36ft models with Duple Commander bodywork in 1964, for Southdown always had an excellent reputation in the coach world, and yet there was PMT running off with this prestigious cup right under Jim's nose!

I was fortunate in having the continued support of my good friend Bob Bailey as Traffic Manager – we had worked happily together in NGT days, quite apart from after my arrival at PMT, which made life much easier, for such long-standing relationships, extending to our respective families, meant that we understood each other and our aims in carrying out the company's policy. However, about 18 months later he was appointed General Manager of Lancashire United Transport Ltd, one of the largest independent operators in the country, so our ways parted again.

While mentioning traffic matters, I must refer to the highly satisfactory relationship we had with the British Railways staff on an informal basis. PMT had been unusual among major bus companies in not having any shareholding by the old railway companies in the days before the latter were nationalised in 1948, so there had been no formal link such as a railway director on the board. Yet despite the informal nature of the contact, a chat over lunch was all that was needed to settle anything, and set up the Stafford bus/rail station, for example. There was no committee until we were more or less instructed to set one up by the Labour Government.

Succeeding me as Chief Engineer was J. D. Mundella, a native of Sunderland but whose earlier career had included two spells with Midland Red. This was the background to his interest in rubber suspension, for among the many advanced engineering ideas that had been adopted in that company was the use of rubber as a suspension medium in co-operation with the Metalastik concern. There was widespread interest in the idea at the time, not least because of its adoption on the Mini car by Alec Issigonis, but Midland Red used it in a different way, putting the rubber in shear and in that case as part of an independent front suspension system. Jim Mundella adapted it with a conventional axles on an AEC Reliance, giving quite promising results, and the idea was taken further later, as I will explain.

In addition to all the problems of running services and the fleet, there was considerable activity on the property side. At Cheadle, we had used a very cramped garage taken over with a local operator's business, but I had the ceremonial duty of cutting the first sod for a much larger garage with booking office built in contemporary style, opening at the end of January 1963. This was in the normal pattern of renewing or replacing old property as the need arose, and just one of many such efforts to improve standards to be found in the bus industry in those days, but sadly all too rare today.

In a quite different league was the replacement of the old open-air bus station at Longton and the garage at Fenton by new premises at Longton, opened in November 1964, which not only provided bus station and garage facilities but included a ten-pin bowling alley. One of BET's ventures into diversification was the ten-pin bowling alley, which had proved a very popular pastime in the United States. Raymond Birch had noted this while on a visit there, and it was decided that the idea of building a bowling alley over a bus

station had considerable potential in that not only was the alley a potentially profitable enterprise in itself but people would use the company's buses to get there and back.

We had an architect's department at PMT, with responsibility for the company's buildings, existing as well as any new work that was in mind, so it fell to it to develop the idea. There was a young man there called Derek Smith and it became his job to pursue the idea. A practical snag we ran into was subsidence. Longton was in an area with coal workings and the differential movement would have meant that the bowling surface was liable to go out of level, clearly not acceptable. So Derek hit on the idea of arranging for the piles driven into the ground to have built-in jacks that would allow the bowling floor to be adjusted.

However, the bowling alley idea was not successful financially and it seems clear that not enough study of the economics was made, especially the very different relationship of costs and disposable income in Longton as compared to the locations used for such centres in the

Keeping on good terms with the local authorities in the area was particularly important in the 'Five Towns'. Here, the Lord Mayor of Stoke is about to climb aboard newly-delivered C916, our first 36ft coach, a Leyland Leopard with Plaxton Panorama bodywork during a visit to our headquarters in 1961. I am standing behind him and, on the right, Bob Bailey, who was Traffic Manager and a good friend since Northern General days, is accompanying the Town Clerk.

Here, the PMT entry in the 1964 British Coach Rally at Brighton, an AEC Reliance with Duple Commander body, is given close examination by the Concours d'Elegance judges. I was particularly pleased that it won the Coach of the Year award, as my predecessor at PMT had moved to become General Manager of Southdown, and this victory was thus on his patch.

United States. Mention should perhaps be made of the name given to this venture – Magnet Bowl, which was a rather clever allusion to the magnet which had been the BET emblem from its early days as well as, perhaps too optimistically, what was hoped to be a magnet for customers.

Ironically there was another structural problem experienced after the bowling alley closed. The premises became a night club and a modest-sized dance floor was provided. Cracks began to appear in the concrete supports of the roof of the bus station below. It turned out that rock and roll music was causing people on the dance floor to pound up and down in a limited area and that this was the cause of the trouble.

In the early 'sixties, we switched to the Daimler Fleetline for our double-deck needs, a feature of the model that particularly appealed being the ability given by the drop-centre rear axle to have centre-gangway layout throughout both decks while retaining the low overall height. It also offered better reliability than the early Atlantean and had the benefit of the Gardner engine with its usual first-class fuel economy and durability. This renewed the contact with Daimler, which by this time had come into the Jaguar group and so I came into contact with Sir William Lyons, a remarkable man with whom I got on well. He had led Jaguar into its strong position in the car industry and who was taking a keen interest in the bus business as a result of Daimler's involvement in it, coupled with the growing success of the Fleetline. Daimler was also fortunate in having Bob Crouch as Sales Director, for he took a genuine interest in the bus operating industry and its needs – indeed, the Fleetline had been based on his assessment of its requirements.

However, that firm's next venture, introduced in 1964, was to prove much less successful. This was the Roadliner rear-engined single-decker. It used a Cummins V6 engine, very compact and quite powerful, which fitted below rear-seat level. Alan Townsin, who is helping me to compile this account of my life, recalls rather ruefully that he described the Roadliner as "the coach driver's dream vehicle" when writing a road test report on a demonstrator example for the technical press, and indeed, its performance and ease of driving were outstanding for the period. Our good experience with the Fleetline, coupled with confidence in both Sir William and Bob Crouch gave what seemed to be good grounds for thinking we were on to a winner. Unfortunately for both Daimler and PMT, the Cummins V6 engine proved to be very troublesome, and was an unhappy introduction of that engine maker, a much respected firm with a position in America quite similar to that of Gardner in Britain, to the bus industry over here – I hear that in more recent years the in-line units by the same maker have proved much more successful.

PMT was looking for a new generation of single-deckers at the time, and with the Fleetline as a generally successful design (even though this partly related to its Gardner engine) the new Daimler single-decker, with its ability to permit a low floor level in bus form, seemed

a good proposition for our needs. The first example to be bodied was completed in PMT red and cream livery and appeared on the Daimler stand at the 1964 Commercial Motor Show. It looked very striking, the Marshall body being to the latest BET style with curved windscreen and rear window. When it entered service, the drivers liked it and, very unusually, the trade union branch wrote an official letter of congratulation to Daimler; the order for 50 we had placed for delivery in 1966-68 seemed well justified. The rubber suspension with which we had experimented was specified for the latter in place of the air suspension used on the prototype.

But then the troubles began. Some with what was effectively a prototype vehicle were not unexpected, but what was worrying was the way they seemed not to respond to attempts to cure them. The engine was the culprit, with overheating, difficulty in starting when hot and smoke emission on stopping service as some of the problems. The delivery of the production batches had not begun before I was given my next appointment, as Deputy General Manager of Midland Red, as described in the next chapter, but PMT struggled on. After the 50 vehicles were delivered, with little improvement in reliability, a subsequent order switched to the Perkins V8 engine which had then become available and was effectively the only alternative that would fit in the limited space. This was rather more successful, but Daimler decided to concentrate on the Fleetline, by then available in single- as well as double-deck form. All in all, the episode was a fiasco, yet the original concept had a lot to be said for it, and if enough effort had been put into getting that engine properly sorted out, it could have been a winner. Vee-form engines are notoriously difficult to get 'right', and many a firm has come to grief over their development, yet the idea of a compact engine that tucks away below the rear seat is a sound one and Mercedes-Benz is just one example of a firm that has succeeded with such a design.

The Daimler Roadliner SRC6 seemed to be a winner at first, but it proved to be quite a nightmare, the problems mainly centred on the Cummins V6 engine mounted at the rear. Here, one of the production vehicles, S1067, dating from 1967 and having Plaxton bodywork, is seen in service.

Chapter Ten: Midland Red

In 1966, apart from the special case of London Transport, Midland Red had the largest bus fleet in the United Kingdom, which of course meant that it was the largest company undertaking. The 'Commercial Motor' analysis of the fleet as it stood on 1st September that year quoted the total as 1,856, down slightly on the previous year's figure of 1,909, in line with the national trend, for the decline from the peak years was under way by then, but still a huge undertaking. Someone had calculated that the operating area covered some 12,000 square miles, with a route mileage of 7,000. Inevitably, its managership was regarded as one of the plum jobs in the industry.

One day while still at PMT, I had a call from John Spencer Wills, at that time BET's Deputy Chairman & Managing Director, though in this context it was very relevant that he was also Midland Red's Chairman. He asked me to come to London and, knowing I was about due for a move, pondered on the implications. I knew that a vacancy at Midland Red would be occurring before too long so inevitably wondered whether it might be offered. Certainly I wanted it. Often in life, success can depend on being in the right place at the right time as well as on being able to do the job.

When I got to Stratton House, the BET headquarters in Piccadilly, Wills said "I want you to join BMMO as Deputy to Donald Sinclair for 12 months with a view to succeeding him." So that was it! The plan was that I would work with and then take over from the immensely respected Donald Sinclair as General Manager on his retirement, due the following year. It was a daunting prospect, yet I would not be honest if I did not say also an exciting one.

Midland Red, or to give its full title of those days, the Birmingham & Midland Motor Omnibus Co Ltd, was yet another company which had its roots in BET's involvement in tramway operation. The story is too complex to explain fully here, but soon after its formation in 1896, the British Electric Traction Co Ltd acquired interests in several tramway companies operating in the area to the west of Birmingham generally known as the Black Country, eventually operating them virtually as one undertaking known as the Birmingham & Midland Tramways. The Birmingham & Midland Motor Omnibus Co Ltd was registered on 26th November 1904, at first as an independent venture, but BET stepped in after very little progress had been made, in 1905. From 1st June that year, it took over fifteen motor buses and also 100 horse buses and some 1,000 horses previously run by BET-owned tramways companies in the area – a bankrupt horse-bus business had been acquired in 1899, and it was this concern that had adopted a red livery for its vehicles from 1900, giving rise to the phrase Midland Red, though in those days it was not part of the company's title. When a fleet name began to be displayed in 1913, it was simply 'Midland', remaining so until my day, even though the company was always generally known as 'Midland Red' and indeed quite frequently 'The Midland Red' in the manner often used for organisations that reached the rank of local institutions in the West Midlands.

The initial attempt at motor bus operation was so much of a flop, mainly because of the problems of maintaining the vehicles in satisfactory repair, that in 1907 it was decided to abandon it and, despite the

When I joined Midland Red, the fleet was still largely composed of 'own make' buses, often of very advanced technical design, though rising costs of small-scale manufacture were causing such a policy to be increasingly uneconomic. No. 5047 was a BMMO S15, a dual-purpose 40-seat vehicle intended mainly for use on the 'X' services linking various Midland cities, seen here awaiting departure time at Nottingham's Mount Street bus station on the X99 to Birmingham. It was one of 48 dating from 1962 which were Midland Red's last 30ft single-deckers. The model, derived from the S14 bus version, was of integral construction, with rubber suspension, independent at the front and weighed under 6 tons, giving good performance with BMMO's own 8-litre engine.

company's name, horse buses only were operated until a more determined venture began in 1912. This time, Tilling-Stevens petrol-electric vehicles were used and these proved much more reliable. From this point, there was no looking back, and expansion soon began. At first operation was concentrated on the Hagley Road and Harborne routes in Birmingham, where there were no tramways. During 1913, routes were started in Smethwick, Oldbury and Sutton Coldfield.

The opening of a tramway along Hagley Road by Birmingham Corporation led to the closing of BMMO bus operation on the same route under the terms of the local licensing arrangements, and eventually to an agreement in February 1914 that BMMO was not to compete with the Corporation's services within the city but was to be permitted to run services between the centre and points outside the boundary over the tram routes, provided there was suitable fare protection to the municipal services. This agreement was still in force in my days with the company, shaping its activities to a considerable extent and indeed similar agreements were common throughout the industry. They could be very irksome, precluding company operation on profitable routes, but did give a stability to the industry and the protection given to the local services helped to ensure that the passengers carried on our services were travelling longer distances .

The company moved its headquarters to Bearwood and soon services were running to Walsall, Coventry, Stratford-upon-Avon, Stourbridge, Redditch, Kidderminster, Great Malvern and Evesham. There were other BET operations in some of the surrounding areas and, partly due to the 1914-18 war, it was agreed that BMMO would operate at first on their behalf, this establishing footholds in Kidderminster, Worcester, Warwick and Nuneaton. By the early 'twenties, BMMO had vehicles operating from Hereford, Bromsgrove, Leamington, Coventry, Stafford and Leicester.

Thus the huge network of routes was gradually built up, and Midland Red became established as the main operator of bus services, apart from the more localised municipal undertakings, within an area which stretched from the Welsh border right over to the East Midlands and included deeply rural areas such as those round Hereford and Banbury. Yet many of these more outlying services were barely profitable even in the best of times and as private motoring developed became steadily more of a burden which was 'carried' by the busier routes in and around the Black Country. The latter became more important as the various BET tramways in the area were gradually abandoned and replaced by Midland Red buses from 1926 onwards, and garages such as Dudley, Oldbury, Cradley Heath and Hartshill as well as those in Birmingham (at Digbeth and Sheepcote Street) and the Bearwood headquarters of those days, grew in size and numbers of vehicles operated. Bearwood was in the borough of Smethwick, which was why Midland Red buses right up to my days with the company always had HA registration numbers. Later, in 1953, the head office was moved to Midland House, 1 Vernon Road, Edgbaston, Birmingham, which was a rather elegant Victorian building conveniently placed in front of Carlyle Works, which had been the overhaul and bus construction works of the company since the 'twenties.

In the early days the company was run in a remarkable way. There was no General Manager, and effectively it was run by O. C. Power, who was Traffic Manager, and L. G. Wyndham Shire, who was Chief Engineer, each reporting to the Chairman based in London. Each became a legendary figure, though of contrasting and sometimes conflicting character. Power had great entrepreneurial flair, especially when opening up new territory, whilst Wyndham Shire had strong ideas about the development of bus design. Each ran their own part of the company almost as if separate organisations. The conductors, part of the traffic staff, came under Power, while the drivers, whose uniforms were different, were under Shire. He came to the conclusion that the Tilling-Stevens petrol-electric bus of the early 'twenties had its limitations, in particular that its performance was too sluggish in relation to the smaller buses used by independent competitors.

The result was Midland Red's own make of bus, originally known as the SOS – the stories of what the initials signified vary, but in many ways the most logical was 'Shire's Own Specification' for he had a flair for getting good results from simple and light designs with lively performance. Early versions were four-cylinder petrol-engined buses, but later six-cylinder models, including a double-decker, were added, and some other BET companies, including both Northern General and Potteries, also used them for a time. By the late 'thirties, an 8-litre diesel engine, with direct injection, had been developed and later versions of this were still to be found in large numbers in the fleet when I arrived on the scene.

In 1940, Wyndham Shire retired and his place was taken by Donald Sinclair, who promptly began work on a new generation of bus, the own-make vehicles by then being usually known by the company's initials, BMMO. He saw the possibilities of the underfloor-engined single-decker and although London Transport had a batch of Green Line coaches, the TF type, built to its requirements on a special Leyland chassis having the engine in this position in 1939, it was Midland Red that showed how, with the entrance ahead of the front axle, a very effective 40-seat design could be produced within the limits of the 27ft 6in length limit of those days. A series of prototypes was built during the war, the first few being conversions of experimental rear-engined vehicles Wyndham Shire had built but not put into production.

Then, in 1943, O. C. Power died and Donald Sinclair was appointed General Manager, though continuing to take a close interest in bus design. The bold step was taken of deciding to standardise on the underfloor-engined bus for all the company's single-deck needs, and the first order for 100 BMMO buses of type S6 was put in hand in 1946, when the major bus manufacturers were still offering only front-engined models. It was not until about 1950 that the major makers such as Leyland and AEC caught up with the pioneer work done by

A batch of 100 Leyland Leopard chassis with bodywork to standardised BET Federation design were placed in service in 1962-3 similar buses were supplied to several other BET companies. Seen here in St Margaret's bus station, Leicester is No. 5205, with 53-seat body by Willowbrook. They proved reliable buses even though less technically advanced than the company's own products.

The Daimler Fleetline was a type I knew from PMT days; No. 5262 seen here in Loughborough was one of Midland Red's first batch, dating from 1963. The Alexander body was of full-height type unlike those supplied to PMT, Midland Red not having routes requiring buses of 'lowbridge' height. The Fleetline proved generally satisfactory in both companies, with good fuel economy from the Gardner 6LX engine, and although there was some transmission and overheating trouble from time to time, it did not reach the epidemic levels found in some city fleets.

The D9 double-decker had more than a little in common with the much-admired London Transport Routemaster – integral construction, independent front suspension, epicyclic gearbox and an all-hydraulic brake system – in addition, there was a 10.5-litre engine, of BMMO's own make, and rubber suspension. As introduced in prototype form in 1958, it also had disc brakes, but they proved unsatisfactory on a vehicle of this weight and drum brakes were substituted. The example shown, No. 5422, was among the last built, dating from 1966. A total of 345 were built, all for the company's own use. In usual Midland Red fashion, weight was modest for a 72-seat 30ft bus, at under 8 tons unladen, and the steel-framed structure did tend to suffer from corrosion in later years.

Midland Red, which by that time had about 300 such buses in use.

Over the years, Midland Red built up a reputation for being at the forefront of new developments in bus design – experiments in and then adoption of integral construction, independent front suspension, disc brakes – you name it, BMMO had done it. Many were remarkably successful, and the S14 single-deck 44-seater put into production in 1954 still sounds advanced almost 40 years later with all the above features and an unladen weight of about 5½ tons. Many of today's midibuses, even the better-quality ones, cannot match so advanced a specification. On the other hand, some things that work well on a vehicle of such weight do not scale up into heavier categories without running into difficulties – there was a famous model engineer who had a saying "you can't scale nature", and it is true, as I found, for the changes in maximum dimensions had created bigger and inevitably heavier buses. Even so, Midland Red was regarded with great respect by the whole operating and manufacturing industry.

So, when I arrived in March 1966, I was conscious of coming to a vast organisation. There were 34 garages and far more people than one could ever get to know on a personal basis, even getting round to meet the local management was no mean task. Yet it had a 'human' quality and, despite its size, the motto 'The friendly Midland Red' was more than just sales talk.

On the vehicle side, the fleet as it stood in September 1966 consisted of 834 double-deckers (729 BMMO of the front-engined D5, D7 and D9 types; the two BMMO D10 underfloor-engined models; 50 Daimler Fleetline and 53 Leyland PD2); 846 single-deck buses (746 BMMO underfloor-engined models, mainly of types S14, S15, S16 and S17, and 100 Leyland Leopard) and 176 coaches (111 BMMO, largely of the various types of C5 including the first and famous CM5 motorway coaches, and the later CM6 series, plus 65 Leyland Leopard).

Thus most of the vehicles in service were of Midland Red's own manufacture, and indeed this was still continuing, though economics were increasingly against it. In one sense, BMMO had been happily placed, with many of the motor industry's major suppliers within a few miles of its works, but an output of about 100 vehicles a year was not really enough to make the manufacture of special parts an economic proposition. In those days, happy in the sense that the vehicle manufacturing industry was booming, suppliers were more interested in much larger quantities and the prices quoted for our type of numbers began to shoot up. In addition, our skilled engineering staff were being tempted away by the high wages obtainable in the car industry, a situation that had other unfortunate consequences, as I will mention later.

It had been decided not to proceed with the idea of the two underfloor-engined D10 double-deckers of 1960-61, although it is ironic to note that a very similar concept in the form of the Volvo double-deck model of much the same layout has been quite successful in recent years. Instead, the Daimler Fleetline had been adopted as the company's double-deck standard, and of course I was familiar with this from my PMT experience. Among single-deck buses and coaches, the Leyland Leopard had proved very successful even if lacking some of the advanced ideas of our own products. Yet even these had run into some difficulties, as I have indicated. Disc brakes had worked well with the light S14 and comparable vehicles but had not proved as effective on larger and heavier buses. The D9 double-decker with its 72 seats weighed a little over 8 tons unladen and began life with disc brakes all round on the prototype, but pad wear proved to be excessive and drum brakes were fitted at the rear on early production examples. Even this did not prove satisfactory and drum brakes were fitted all round latterly, earlier buses being converted.

Donald Sinclair had run the company with great success for over 20 years, but his health was beginning to fail, partly as a consequence of pressure due to his wife's illness, and he no longer had the energy and drive of earlier years, immensely skilled and experienced though he was. Senior officers of the company, sometimes lacking clarity of direction from above, were doing their own thing to some degree, and the whole thing had to be given a sense of purpose once more.

Shortages of staff

The mid-sixties were a period of virtually full employment, and one of the main problems was that of retaining staff, particularly as there was considerable time and cost devoted to staff training which had to be undertaken all over again when people left, sometimes to use the skills they had gained with us for the benefit of others. The car industry had grown immensely, and while this had a very beneficial effect on the health of the local economy in the West Midlands, and some on the demand for travel on our buses, it also was beginning to create serious problems.

The trade unions had amassed immense power in the car plants, most notably at the Longbridge factory of the Austin concern, by then part of what was called the British Motor Corporation, and then from 1968, the British Leyland Motor Corporation. They were exploited by politically motivated forces which had destructive aims in view, as became clear when the extent to which communist connections of some of the more notorious trade union activists to the KGB in Soviet Russia were confirmed by revelations made in more recent years. This had a spin-off effect, since the lure of high wages at Longbridge drew staff away from other employers, including BMMO. This was particularly so for engineering staff and keeping enough fitters was becoming well-nigh impossible.

This helped to make manufacture of our own vehicles even more expensive, and the decision was made to phase this out. Double-deck output was ceasing at about the time I arrived, with the last of the D9 models, of advanced technical design, with their integral construction, independent front suspension, 10-litre

Midland Red's integral single-deck designs, still with rubber suspension, independent at the front, were developed to take advantage of the 36ft (11-metre) length permissible from 1961, seating 52 in bus form. The initial version, S16, retained the 8-litre engine and manual gearbox of earlier types, but the S17 had the 10.5-litre, similar to that in the D9 but in horizontal form, and a semi-automatic epicyclic gearbox, and yet its weight was only just over 6½ tons. A total of 262 were built between 1963 and 1966, when the vehicle seen here in Shrewsbury, No.5740, was one of the final batch of this type.

BMMO engine, semi-automatic transmission. On the other hand, they retained the rear-entrance layout, which meant that they could not be converted to one-man operation, which was to become important later, so maybe it was just as well we stopped.

The single-deck models carried on up to 1970, though in reducing numbers, and indeed the decision to cease production was not made public until 1969, though the writing had been on the wall for some time before that. The final types, all 36ft (11-metre) long, were the S21 and S22 dual-purpose types and the S23 bus version. These also had the 10-litre engine, in horizontal form, mounted amidships under the floor, as on all Midland Red single-deckers since 1946. Semi-automatic gearboxes were standard on these, too – many operators were finding that clutch life on buses of this length with conventional gearboxes operating in urban conditions was poor, and the fluid flywheel with Wilson-type epicyclic box in its form with direct selection of the gears by a miniature switch was proving a better proposition. The problem was that in traffic, perhaps at a roundabout, drivers would find themselves in the 'wrong' gear and then find their hands too busy steering the bus to change gear, attempting to cope by slipping the clutch, causing rapid wear.

However, as big a problem from the point of view of providing reliable services was the shortage of fitters at garages, creating problems soon to create a crisis for the company. Indeed, there was a general shortage of staff, which not only meant that it was quite often difficult to find crews to cover services but also that it was almost impossible to enforce discipline.

Say anything to a slack employee and he could simply get another job, quite often better paid, in the generally prosperous motor industry which, despite frequent strikes, at that stage was not feeling the effects of competition from imports to any significant extent –

Japanese cars were still very rare and even French or German by no means common. It was not simply the giant car factories such as Austin at Longbridge and Standard-Triumph and the Rootes group, making Hillman and Humber cars in the Coventry area, or even the specialist firms such as Jaguar or Daimler, also in Coventry, but all the firms which supplied the major producers, particularly thick on the ground in Birmingham and the Black Country and hence on our doorstep.

When first I arrived, there were trade union problems, with a strike every Saturday for weeks on end, the situation not being helped by the fact that the main union involved was the Transport & General Workers Union, which was also the main source of trouble in the car industry, as its membership included many of the production workers at places like Longbridge. That is not to condemn the more responsible type of active trade unionist, for fortunately for Midland Red there was always a solid core of the old traditional type of busman, who would turn out for duty regardless of the weather at perhaps 5am and worked on the principle that the bus must get through. But inevitably, there was some influence from the politically motivated hot-heads within the TGWU organisation – it has always been a 'difficult' union, quite often to the detriment of its members.

Overshadowing the whole picture was the wider political scene. A General Election in October 1964 resulted in the return of a Labour Government, for the first time since 1951. It had only a small majority and at first trod carefully in regard to transport matters – too carefully for the views of the more militant members of the Party and in particular the TGWU, which had a powerful voice in policy matters in those days. So the mild Tom Fraser was replaced by the fiery Barbara Castle as Minister of Transport just before Christmas

1965. The battle over the question of nationalisation of the bus industry was back again, in much the same way as it had been in 1947-50. Mrs Castle had strong left-wing views, and there was no doubt of her commitment to public ownership. On the other hand, she was not prepared to swallow the idea of simply carrying on with the process of building up a set-up like the British Transport Commission directly responsible for transport across the whole country, as had been planned then, and as many in the unions expected.

She was influenced, perhaps rather surprisingly, by American ideas, for there had been a revival of interest there in public bodies that would run public transport in and around major cities. Her original proposals for similar bodies for this country were called Conurbation Transport Authorities – 'conurbation' was a much-used word at that time, referring to areas of which the West Midlands, comprising Birmingham and the surrounding densely-populated and largely industrial area, was an obvious example, and indeed there was a specific proposal for that area.

Quite apart from the fact that many of Midland Red's most important services ran within the proposed area and were thus under threat, there was also the implications for the principle of cross-subsidy which was woven into the structure of many major bus companies across the country, including Midland Red. Even in the most profitable days for bus operation, there had been no money to be made in the more deeply rural areas, simply because not enough people travelled to cover the costs of even the most basic service. At that time, the idea of directly subsidising services out of the public purse was unknown in Britain. Essential services in rural areas were supported by the profits made on busier routes, and the need for such internal support was taken into account by the Traffic Commissioners in considering applications for licences for new services, for example.

Naturally, my thoughts went back to those days of anti-nationalisation when I was with Northern General and of course BET was still very much a private-enterprise organisation. John Spencer Wills, who had

meanwhile become Chairman of BET as well as continuing in that role for Midland Red, saw the whole picture in the same way, so I felt quite clear that we had to fight the proposals head on. So once again I found myself organising campaigns against the new proposals.

Smaller operators were also opposed to the Government's ideas, and this time a more effective common front was set up. I arranged for meetings to which the local and national press were invited, and among the independent operators' representatives who joined us in presenting our case was Ron Whittle, of J. W. Whittle & Sons of Highley, near Kidderminster, someone for whom I soon gained great respect. His company was best known in those days for its impressive coach fleet, almost completely renewed on an annual basis. This was quite a remarkable achievement, only made possible by shrewd deals under which the displaced vehicles were taken in part exchange and, in turn, sold on to other operators at good prices. It became known among smaller independents that ex-Whittle coaches were good buys, and at one time it was quite common to find them still running in their original colours for a while, though not on their own patch. It was a phenomenon of the times, when coach excursion and holiday business prospered and the lightweight type of coach on a Bedford or Ford chassis was relatively cheap to buy, yet had good resale value over its early years. Whittle did offer to sell out to Midland Red, but the fleet structure did not fit, and the firm remained independent and indeed prospered, though in different ways, branching out into new activities such as participation in a service to London when deregulation made this possible.

The campaign continued, as did Mrs Castle's efforts. Spencer Wills sent me over to the United States to have a look at the Massachusetts Bay Transit Authority, which was believed to be one of the models on which she based her thinking. I was not impressed, and set about preparing a report to that effect. The ideas for the conurbations became more clear-cut, the name changing to Passenger Transport Authorities, which would be the policy-making bodies, formed largely by nominees of

In the campaign against nationalisation, we made strong use of the motorway coach service which had made Midland Red quite famous. Here I am taking the opportunity to talk to passengers boarding at Digbeth on the service to London. Welcome support was being given by Ron Whittle, of one of the largest independent operators in the area, wearing the light suit, who had soon proved an able and effective ally in the campaign. The picture is dated August 1967 and, unbeknown to me, there had already been contact between the Government and BET with a view to the latter selling its bus interests. It was rejected at first, but by November agreement had been reached, coming as a huge shock to me.

The London Motorway service coaches carried slogans to convey the anti-nationalisation message. Here one of the CM6T coaches which replaced the original 1959 motorway service fleet in 1965-6 bears the lettering 'Help us retain the service of your choice'. These displays were still in use as the news came through of the sale of BET's bus interests to THC, putting me in a very embarrassing position. These coaches, like their predecessors, had been designed before the 70mph speed limit was introduced, and had run safely at well over that figure.

the local authorities in the area, with Passenger Transport Executives reporting to them, composed of professionals who would run the services and own the fleets. However, there was strong pressure from the unions for action outside the urban areas, with direct pressure for the take-over of BET. An approach was made around the beginning of 1967 to see whether BET would simply sell, rather as the Tilling group had done back in 1948. Back in those days, BET had stood firm, and at least partly this was on the basis that virtually all of its bus activities were profitable, some highly so. In 1967, the picture was less clear-cut, for the reasons I have outlined, but the answer was still "no". I questioned Spencer Wills two or three times but continued to get the same answer. I sent in my report on the Massachusetts Bay scheme, though by the time it was done, the attitude at BET headquarters was changing, though we in the operating companies were unaware of this.

So of course we battled on, knowing that the dice were loaded against us – a General Election in April 1966 had resulted in an increased Labour majority. The motorway coaches that had made Midland Red quite famous carried slogans such as "Help us to maintain the service of your choice". Yet behind the scenes, more talks were being held in London. The British Transport Commission had been dismantled by the Conservative Government in 1962, and so far as its bus interests were concerned had been replaced by the Transport Holding Company, still State-owned, which acted as the parent body of the Tilling and Scottish Bus companies and of course held the ex-BTC shares in BET companies such as Midland Red.

So it was through THC that negotiations were conducted. Mrs Castle's published diaries reveal that she invited both John Spencer Wills and Sir Reginald Wilson, Deputy Chairman and Managing Director of THC to lunch in May, revealing her plans for powers of compulsory acquisition of non-PTE operators' services within the PTE areas. This was unbeknown to me, of course, and I was holding one of the Midland Red protest meetings in company with independent operators

that same month! At BET headquarters the whole situation was coming under review, though understandably no word was passed down to those of us at 'the battle front', even when serious negotiation for a purchase of BET's bus interests by THC got under way. At that stage it became a matter of trying to secure the best price and it would not have done for any hint or rumour to give the impression that BET had 'given in'. In fact, unwittingly I was doubtless helping by ensuring that Midland Red remained very vocal in opposing any idea of nationalisation. This situation continued right through that summer and autumn, until it was announced on 22nd November that an offer of £35 million had been agreed, which covered BET's shareholdings which gave control of companies running about 11,000 buses, thereby opening the door to the creation of the National Bus Company by adding this to the Tilling companies already in State ownership.

The whole thing came as quite a shock, though fortunately I was given about an hour's private warning by Tony West, BET's public relations man, a former newspaper journalist who had played quite a prominent part in the coordination of our local efforts and with whom I had worked quite closely. So when Wills phoned me, I was able to avoid reacting with quite the full horror I might well have done without having been tipped off.

Even so, we were all being asked to change the political direction from that we had followed throughout our careers in the company bus business almost as swiftly as if a sergeant-major on a long route march had suddenly shouted "About Turn". It took a little time not only to kill the momentum of the anti-nationalisation campaign but to think through the full implications of the new situation. One thing was certain – it did little if anything to solve Midland Red's huge problems and we were in for a rough time during the next few years, when the harsh facts of life began to be made clear to us all and not least the politicians, of whatever persuasion, who thought they knew all the answers.

Chapter Eleven: Operation Phoenix

The National Bus Company took over the Transport Holding Company's bus interests in England and Wales, including its ex-BET subsidiaries, on 1st January 1969. At Midland Red, quite a major crisis was blowing up and although its direct causes were a combination of factors that had been building up for some time, including several mentioned in the last chapter, the experience underlined the way in which a political 'solution' has remarkably little effect when hard economics intervene.

On the face of things, the economic climate, both nationally and especially in the West Midlands, was good, with what would nowadays be regarded as almost negligible unemployment – the figures mostly related to people who were 'between jobs' for a few weeks at most. The motor industry was dominant in its effect on local well-being not only within the major factories building cars and other vehicles in Birmingham and Coventry but also keeping busy numerous ancillary businesses, large and small, especially in the Black Country served very largely by our buses. At that date, the effects of competition from abroad were still quite small, and although the car industry in particular was convulsed with increasing frequency by strikes the overall pattern was one of growing prosperity, as had been so in the area for 20 years or so. In one sense, this worked against us, for car workers could buy new cars on very advantageous terms and even where this did not apply, the relatively high wages helped to allow more people to own cars, still by no means universal in other comparable industrial areas, and once they did, they used the buses less.

On the basis of the general prosperity of the area, it had seemed that the fleet might grow to 2,000 buses, which would have been an impressive landmark. In some undertakings, especially the municipal ones, size of fleet was regarded as a measure of prestige for the management and their rates of pay were sometimes based on fleet size. We had to take a much more hard-nosed view, State-owned though we were. It was Derek Fytche, who had joined me, initially as Traffic Manager soon after I was appointed as General Manager, who quickly spotted that this was the wrong direction to be going and that in fact it needed reducing and using more intensively to make an attack on costs. He was to be a tower of strength in getting to grips with what needed to be done to bring the company round from what proved to be a near disaster.

There was also the effect of the seemingly thriving motor industry on recruitment, and perhaps more especially, the tendency for staff to be attracted away from the bus operating business, with its unsocial hours and increasingly limited ability to match fast-rising rates of pay elsewhere. It was fair to say that the latter were inflated and indeed were beginning to build into quite alarming rates of national inflation, reducing the value of money and triggering yet more strikes for more pay, but that didn't alter the position when a hitherto loyal and hard-working employee, not necessarily skilled in engineering, had been tempted by the good pay available at say the huge Longbridge works south of Birmingham, founded by Austin but by then part of the British Motor Corporation and then the British Leyland Motor Corporation.

The latter was yet another manifestation of the turmoil in the organisation of major enterprises and had been formed in 1968. At that stage it was not State-owned, though it had been encouraged by the Labour Government, but the merger of the Leyland empire with the larger but far less sound BMC was another recipe for disaster in the long run. It also created something very close to a monopoly in bus supply, for Daimler and Guy had been taken over by Jaguar Cars, and in turn this group had merged with BMC (which was mainly Austin and Morris) in an effort to gain bigger reserves of capital for expansion. With Leyland already in control of AEC and Albion and its shareholding link with Bristol and Eastern Coach Works (these latter two having been almost the sole suppliers to the ex-Tilling operating companies now our partners within NBC), heavy-duty bus supply had come into one group, with obvious dangers from the operators' viewpoint.

In Midland Red's case, this almost coincided with the run-down of its own bus manufacturing facilities and this underlined the contrast between designing our buses to suit our needs and having to deal with the now all-powerful Leyland concern. In fact, this situation, with opportunities as well as dangers, led to the setting-up of the Leyland National Company, announced in July 1969 as to be jointly owned by Leyland and NBC to build the integral-construction single-decker of that name, and the bringing of Bristol and ECW into a new 50-50 relationship as part of the same set-up. In due course, Midland Red was to receive some of the first production examples in 1972, which brought their own headaches, but meanwhile we had plenty of other problems and so far as BLMC's bus manufacturing side was concerned, our biggest immediate one was an alarming shortage of spare parts, which aggravated growing difficulties in keeping buses in good order largely caused by the problems of maintenance staff shortage. Practical considerations led to some of the more adventurous features of BMMO-built buses being altered to improve service life. Thus disc brakes, notably

The decision to cease Midland Red's manufacture of its own buses had been taken well before it became part of NBC, but the wind-down was gradual, so the last examples did not enter service until 1970. The final type was the S23, as seen in this view of one of the final batch, No.5958 bound for Wellington on the X94 route. Towards the end, the type numbers became quite complex, and mechanically the last types, S21, 22 and 23 were generally similar to the S17 shown on page 61, but the body shell was derived from that of the CM6 coaches. The S21 and S22 were both dual-purpose, but the S23 were 51-seat buses, equipped from new to allow one-man operation. The last 50, including this bus, had bodywork completed by Plaxton, at Scarborough.

So ended a remarkable era, stretching back to 1923, when BMMO had begun producing its own bus chassis with the original SOS Standard or S-type. Over the years, many advances in design had been pioneered, often well before they had been taken up by commercial manufacturers, but changes in economics were working against what was relatively small-scale manufacture.

The Leyland Leopard had been favoured for part of Midland Red's single-deck bus and coach needs from 1962, and No. 6143 was one of fifteen on the shorter PSU4 chassis added to the fleet in 1969 and designated LC10 within the company. The 36-seat body was by Plaxton to its Panorama Elite design with curved side windows then newly in production. Such vehicles were useful for touring work, then an important Midland Red activity and on which the firm had built up a first-class reputation. The Leopard was a very reliable machine, these later examples having semi-automatic Pneumocyclic gearboxes which made the driver's job easier than the synchromesh gearbox of the earlier versions and gave little trouble in this application.

on the D9 double-deckers, were replaced by drum, and in some cases rubber suspension was replaced by steel springs.

But it was the effects on staffing of the local employment situation in 1969 that first began to ring the alarm bells for Midland Red. The loss of staff became such that service reliability began to suffer noticeably because there were not enough drivers or conductors to run all the scheduled journeys. At that stage, we were part-way through the process of converting to one-man operation as it was almost always still called, and the majority of double-deckers were still of rear-entrance type and thus had to have a crew of two. A productivity scheme introduced after talks with the unions that year made a temporary improvement in the situation.

Then the shortage of maintenance staff, also worsening and a particular problem because of the big demand for engineering skills in the area, began to become the dominant factor. We had the ironic situation that even if we had crews, serviceable vehicles were too few for the workings which could otherwise have been run. Being reduced to working hand-to-mouth in this way had wider consequences. Not only did the general state of the fleet suffer when staff could not be spared to rectify minor but non-disabling defects if needed to attend to some task which would put a bus back into service, but more fundamental duties were being neglected.

The ultimate nightmare of any transport manager came when one of our buses, parked temporarily on sloping ground in the bus station at Dudley with the engine running, ran away downhill and killed a pedestrian. It seems that the handbrake ratchet failed, perhaps due to vibration from the idling engine shaking it loose. The circumstances left unanswered the question as to whether the brake had been applied firmly enough and the engine stopped or other steps taken to prevent the risk of runaway when parking on a gradient. The fact remained that the ratchet was worn and whether or not this was the true cause of the accident, it was inevitable that it set off a close investigation of the remaining vehicles belonging to Dudley garage by the Ministry of Transport inspector, and several were put under PSV71 prohibition notices, banning their use until repaired.

Anyone with experience of bus maintenance will know that the type of defect that can be picked up in this way may not be as dramatic as this sounds – indeed I suspect that quite a high proportion of private cars would collect such notices if subjected to similarly rigorous standards, which can cover matters relating to the state of the vehicle's seating, for example, and not merely obvious 'safety' items. Even so, it was a shattering experience, and to have any of one's vehicles involved in a fatal accident is bad enough without any question of a mechanical defect being a contributory factor. Yet the whole episode was a dramatic manifestation of the wider question of staff shortage already mentioned.

Drastic measures had to be taken, and in particular a very careful check on safety items. One of my practices in going round garages was to go straight to the drivers'

defect sheets which gave a very good indication of whether we were coping or not. However, a more extensive and rigorous examination revealed a number of other defects that might have led to dangerous situations if not picked up, and I have to say I wonder about the wisdom of the modern trend towards reducing the provision of engineering facilities among some of today's operators. Some work was farmed out to private car repair garages, leading to the unprecedented situation of a modern double-deck bus from the biggest bus company in the country being seen among cars awaiting attention at a local motor repairers. The episode had a good effect in that it forced the issue of ensuring that engineering standards could not be allowed to drop, even if money was tight.

Then the emphasis went back to a traffic staff shortage, caused this time by the effects of the revised drivers' hours regulations which came into effect in March 1970. This time quite unbelievable unreliability of service resulted from the inability to allow drivers to work as much overtime as had been the only way of keeping services going hitherto. Clearly, no responsible operator would want to put safety in jeopardy, but the new regulations were very complex and had been introduced without adequate consideration of their effects, which were often quite ludicrous, something which was at least partially conceded later when they were modified.

At the time, however, we were in very serious trouble, with a loss of scheduled operating mileage of up to 10 per cent. This was an average figure covering the company as a whole, but where the staff shortages were worst, passengers were literally faced with a situation where it could be no more than a 50-50 chance of a scheduled bus appearing. This had a doubly disastrous effect, for not only the fares of the passengers thus let down were lost but the lack of reliability led them to seek other means of making their journeys, generally by car and thus leading to recurring losses of custom.

It was hardly surprising that passenger travel dropped by 10 per cent over the year. Revenue dropped by £502,000, while expenditure rose by £738,000 over the estimates made at a fares increase hearing granted early in the year. Thus an estimated operating surplus of £572,000 became an actual loss of £669,000. It became essential for another fares increase application to be made, the third in little over a year, leading to sharp political criticism from both Labour and Conservative M.P.s as well as local councils. We were in deep trouble on several fronts.

This major financial crisis was seen as something quite new. Up to the mid-'sixties, it had been taken for granted that bus undertakings could be profitable. Indeed, even the ground rules for NBC, laid down as a reflection of the decidedly left-wing socialist philosophy of Barbara Castle as Minister of Transport, assumed that it would pay its way to the extent that it was required to make annual payments to the Government. These were equivalent in many ways to the dividends from a profitable company, but with no provision for its relief

Stratford Blue had been an independent company acquired by Midland Red in 1935, but it was not absorbed and was run as a separate business. It had its own vehicle policy, not using BMMO vehicles but standardising on production Leyland types from 1948 and having its own distinctive blue and cream livery. In BET days such companies were used in the career development process, management gaining experience and confidence in a small concern before graduating to larger ones. However, in the earlier NBC era, the trend was towards larger units and Stratford Blue was absorbed into Midland Red from January 1971. Here, two Leyland Titans are seen in March of that year, No. 19, a PD3/4 dating from 1960, still in the blue livery while on the right, a PD3A/1 of 1963, had become Midland Red No. 2002 – both had Willowbrook bodywork.

in the eventuality that it might make a loss – indeed, this requirement was to prove so harsh as to create major problems for NBC.

Looking back with the benefit of hindsight, it seems amazing that there was no provision for such a situation in the legislation, for there was plenty of evidence of mounting problems as the profitability of the industry had long past its peak. Yet the company side of the industry had depended for its existence on being commercially viable and the big groups like BET, and even the Tilling group, State-owned since 1948, had a long history of success without subsidy, so what was to prove a false sense of confidence had been built up. Almost all the major operating companies had some loss-making routes, even in the days of peak travel demand in the early post-war years, but it was accepted practice that these could be carried by the profitable ones, and indeed the Traffic Commissioners expected the territorial companies responsible for most of the services in their area to adopt this approach.

In fact, for most companies there had been a general decline in passengers carried since some time in the 'fifties. So revenue tended to drop unless fares were raised. Costs, and in particular wages, had been going up at the same time, at first fairly slowly, so fares had to be raised to counteract this too. We had been in a pattern of regular, usually annual, fares increases for many years and, in those days, an application for an increase in fares had to be submitted to the Traffic Commissioners with the justifying evidence in terms of cost before it would be approved and could be put into effect.

All this, followed by the recasting of fare tables each time, was a huge job in a big company like Midland Red, and the process, with the involvement of the Traffic Commissioners' staff at the various stages, took several months, causing the hoped-for increase in revenue to be well behind the increases in costs which made it

necessary. As inflation began to worsen, this effect became more marked, magnified by the way in which higher fares and poorer services simply led to yet more loss of custom, and we were right in the firing line in the Midlands with the motor industry constantly setting the pace for higher wages.

Some pretty drastic action had to be taken, and we christened it 'Operation Phoenix'. I was very fortunate in the team I had around me, not only in terms of my senior officers in Birmingham, for the company's Chairmen gave immensely valuable help and moral support. When BET sold its bus interests, John Spencer Wills naturally stayed with the group of which he had become Chairman, so his chairmanship of Midland Red became vacant. The first to hold the position under the nationalised regime was Frank Pointon, one of only three BET Executive Directors who decided to move over with the buses. He was appointed West Midland Regional Chairman under NBC's initial organisation, but of course I had known him for years in BET days. Like all of us, he was brought up in the tradition of buses paying their way, and I remember him well saying to me when the bad financial picture emerged "Walter, we mustn't get used to these 'loss' figures, no, we must not", and indeed I agreed completely with this sentiment. As we got Phoenix under way, I put out an edict, saying "We are going to break even this year, one way or another", as a starting point before getting back into profit.

To achieve this, I could see that we would have to further reduce the size of the fleet by 100 buses and at one of our Monday morning meetings of senior officers, I raised the matter with James Isaac, who had become Traffic Manager in October 1969, enabling Derek Fytche to take a broader view of the company's activities as Deputy General Manager. James Isaac incidentally came to the company from North Western and I said to him "Jim, we've got to have another 100 vehicles out of the fleet to make this work". "No way", he said, "can't be done" – and although these weekly meetings had no agenda, so he'd had no chance to bone up on the implications, James was always a man who knew his stuff, having rapidly built up an immensely detailed knowledge of the company's whole operations in his head, so his reaction wasn't said lightly. But I knew it was vital, so I said "James, I have never given an order since I left the forces, but I am giving one now. You will do it and I will take complete responsibility". Of course, in later years, he rose to the top rank in the profession, becoming Director General of West Midlands PTE and still as I write Chairman of its successor West Midlands Travel Ltd, but I know he told the story everywhere, and I don't blame him!

In fact, we were all busy working to turn things round. An important step was the productivity deal announced in April 1970, which introduced the basic principle of five-day duties covering the Monday to Friday period, with optional working at weekends. This was intended to put work on the buses on a more competitive basis with industry in general. The rates of pay were 10s (50p) per hour for the first 40 hours of work, 12s 5d (62p) for anything over this on Mondays to Fridays and 14s (70p) for Saturdays and Sundays. These figures hardly sound impressive 24 years later after further periods of inflation, but they were enough to bring a driver's pay with various bonuses up to £35 per week, which did much in itself to rectify the recruitment problem.

It was part of an agreement which gave important freedoms, possibly the most important being able to employ part-time staff, hitherto strongly opposed by the unions, but they could see the logic in the circumstances of the time. Some of these were retired drivers and others were office or other employees not usually on driving duties but which held p.s.v. drivers' licences. There were about 360 by 1971, and among them five women drivers, then quite rare, though Midland Red had had several during the 1939-45 war. As a result of these measures, service reliability greatly improved, scheduled service rose to 99-100 per cent during the week and 98 per cent at week-ends.

Derek Fytche was also busy around this time on some research work on vehicle scheduling being carried out by Leeds University as a joint project with International Computers involving Bristol Omnibus as well as Midland Red. Such duties had been very time-consuming and big savings in clerical time as well as important gains in the ability to respond to changing needs for services were shown to be possible. This was another instance of how we were at the cutting edge not only in experiencing problems but in developing answers to them.

On the vehicle side, Ray Braithwaite joined the company as Chief Engineer at the beginning of 1970 from the equivalent post with Northern General Transport, on the retirement of Eric Tuff. His task was indeed a daunting one, turning the fleet round from a low ebb that had built up because of the staff position. This again responded to productivity schemes both at the central Carlyle Works and the operating garages, but even with adequate staff getting a run-down fleet back up to an efficient standard takes time even with the most efficient methods, another point to be borne in mind today when operators have been driven to delay normal replacement programmes because of financial problems arising from unregulated competition.

However, Midland Red as it stood at that date had a wide variety of operating conditions, from intensive urban services as tough as any in city fleets around Birmingham to deep rural operation in, say, Herefordshire. We benefited from the adoption of an idea used in several of the ex-Tilling NBC fleets, where maintenance was governed by fuel consumed rather than mileage covered. The same type of bus might return say 8mpg in Birmingham and 11mpg on a country route, and by linking a service to the consumption of 300 gallons, the mileages would be 2,400 and 3,300 respectively. This also had the effect of picking up a bus that was using more fuel than it should, implying sub-standard engine and quite probably general condition, for more frequent attention until it could be brought up to standard at overhaul. This used the company computer and similar ideas were applied to other engineering work – it proved possible to increase the output of overhauled engines and units from Carlyle Works by 40 per cent, this playing a big part in getting the fleet back up to proper standards. Needless to say, safety received particular attention, with a 45-point check list applied at about 3,000-mile intervals.

Tackling morale

Amid all this practical work, there was the important matter of morale to tackle. There can be nothing more damaging to the mood within a company than for the staff to see it being criticised by the public it seeks to serve and meets every day as well as by politicians and by the media. Transport companies are particularly vulnerable to this and, right back to my Army days, I've always been conscious of how important it was to keep the morale of the troops up. Midland Red had an old-established staff bulletin which I felt was very important. Its style had not altered for many years and, in some ways, I was loth to change it, for tradition is important in a firm like Midland Red.

However, a familiar friend came on the scene. Tony West, whom I'd got to know well because of his involvement in the anti-nationalisation campaigns, had not felt happy with the NBC as originally set up, and for a little while went to pastures new. He was running a public relations firm in Yorkshire and in 1970 Frank Pointon asked him to come to a meeting with Derek Fytche and me, and it was agreed that a programme to improve management-staff relations be put in hand. Tony felt strongly that the staff bulletin had to be completely revamped. I was reluctant, but eventually agreed.

Of course he was right, and the first new-style

Gaining and keeping the confidence of the staff in a big and widely spread organisation like Midland Red was crucial, especially when the company was beset with problems. I had always valued the staff bulletin, but was advised that its very traditional design was holding it back from having the impact needed. Here 'old' and 'new' covers of issues from September-October 1969 and March-April 1971 are compared – the press cutting on the latter was of an article on resistance to the proposed take-over of Midland Red services within the West Midlands PTE area but the headline was true of the feeling within the company as it coped with a combination of problems.

bulletin duly appeared in September 1970. It broke new ground among its contemporaries in including a column written by the then District Organiser of the Transport and General Workers' Union, Ken Coleclough. The TGWU was very militant in those days, yet I had found that when we got down to talking, it was possible to understand each others' viewpoints and hammer out agreements of benefit to both sides – the productivity deals proved the point. Ken Coleclough was free to make constructive criticism of the company, the only limitation on what he wrote was that his column must not be used to call for industrial action against the company. I am sure this was to our benefit – it helped to rebuild the team spirit and that was vital.

As it turned out, Frank Pointon was not to continue his chairmanship of Midland Red long enough to see the full result of the fight-back, being given responsibility for the Southern area of NBC under a reorganisation from January 1971 and later, in 1977-81, becoming Deputy Chief Executive. In his place, Ian Patey was appointed to become what was now Regional Chairman, Midlands, and although our earlier careers had followed different tracks, he being an ex-Tilling man, he brought valuable experience as well as great strength of character and devotion to duty. Indeed he was a man above men in my book.

He had been General Manager of the Bristol Omnibus Co Ltd, one of Tilling's biggest and most prestigious companies, and one with more urban operation than most in that group, so he had a shrewd idea from personal experience of the nature of many of our problems. Then he had been Regional Director in Yorkshire before taking on the Midlands. He lived on Hayling Island, near Portsmouth, where he had started his career as an accountant yet was generally in his office in London by 7.30 or 8.00am, so his was no leisurely life even at high seniority and an age when many are looking to taking life a little easier.

As the crisis went on, he said "you know, Walter, you are not going to make this break even". I said "I know all about that – for that's what they keep telling me". The Treasury, of all people had become involved, and they brought in a firm of Canadian accountants to go right through everything. They spent long sessions with my senior officers going through all the figures, but using a different format. They also had a quite different way of forecasting and spent months with us and in the end came to the conclusion that we were not going to break even but would lose another million pounds! Of course this went straight to the Ministry, and I was sent for to go to a meeting with Jim Skyrme at NBC headquarters – this would be about August 1971, the financial year end being in December.

Ian Patey rang me up when we were in all this trouble and a regional Board meeting was to be held, said "Now then Walter, we need a pre-Board meeting. What time could you be down here in London?" I was in Birmingham, of course. I said "When are you in the office?" I had to, of course, but I think he appreciated the point. So I was down there for 8am. After we'd talked, he said "Have you ever been to a Christy's wine tasting?" I told him that I hadn't, so he said "Let's go", and we went across by bus. He was a great wine man, going to France and all over Europe, buying it and selling it all round. It took a while to get round, sampling what was on offer and there was only enough time to grab a sandwich before the Board meeting. I don't think George Brook, who was Regional Director, was too impressed, but we held the meeting and it went quite well.

Clearly, however, the prospect of the meeting with Skyrme had every sign of being much more daunting, and indeed I could visualise that it seemed likely to be

Computers had just begun to play a significant part in the management of major concerns in the 'sixties, and Midland Red was one of the first bus operating companies to have its own installation, seen here. I was glad of the precise and up-to-date information it gave me in getting the company back into the black in 1971. In later years, this became the headquarters of NBC Computer Services Ltd, playing an important part in developing the Market Analysis Project method of designing bus services to give the most efficient patterns of operation.

an awful experience, with me sitting in the hottest of hot seats. However, Midland Red was one of the first firms in the business to have a powerful computer, and just before I left for the meeting we had had it working day and night on the whole situation, and I was able to get a print-out which indicated that we were just about going to break even on a graph it produced. So I was able to arrive at this meeting with this print-out. Jim Skyrme, having listened to what I said, turned to Ian Patey and asked him what he thought. Bless him, he simply said "I back this forecast if Womar says so".

The meeting broke up and we went upstairs to the Mess for lunch, Patey said to me "Of course you know you can't do it, don't you?" He was a great cost man and didn't half know his stuff on finance. I said, "What do you bet me?" He said "I'll bet you 10-1 you can't break even at the end of the year". I said "I'll take it in fivers!"

It got to about November, and he said again "You know you are not going to do it." I said "No I don't, what's the betting now?" He said "I won't give you 10-1 but I'll make it 5-1." So I stood to gain £75 or lose £15. So it came to 17th December and all the signs were that we'd done it, so Patey conceded, not only sending me the money but adding a case of wine, which was in character. In the event, we made £120,000 profit, confounding the 'experts' once again.

It was an important victory, yet there was still a cloud hanging over the company – indeed it had been there since the setting up of the new structure for the industry as a result of the 1968 Transport Act. The West Midlands Passenger Transport Executive had come into operation in October 1969, immediately taking over the former municipal bus undertakings of Birmingham (itself nearly as big as Midland Red), Walsall, Wolverhampton and West Bromwich.

Not only did this create a giant new operator on our doorstep, for far more significant were the powers it had been given to take charge of all public passenger transport within its area, which took in the whole of the industrial and residential area of Birmingham and the Black Country – almost all our most profitable territory! It was required to come to an agreement with NBC over how

this was to be done but the threat was there from the beginning that this might amount to a take-over.

This became specific and public early in 1971, just as we were struggling to rebuild our good name. There was the hope some deal allowing us to continue, perhaps acting as operating agent for the PTE, but the latter proved to be determined that it was to be a straightforward takeover of all those Midland Red operations which were entirely within the PTE area. Quite apart from the obvious direct loss of what was effectively the heart of Midland Red, the viability of what was left was put in grave doubt. I have explained how the principle of cross-subsidy had enabled loss-making rural services to survive, and now there was to be little if anything from which to draw the money to do so. Indeed, even with the company's operating area still intact, we had been forced by the financial pressures to curtail many rural services and withdraw some altogether.

Admittedly the 1968 Act did include new provisions for the support of rural services by direct subsidy from the county councils, but this was something entirely new, and rural counties had no inclination to provide such support, nor the expertise to administer their new involvement in deciding what services needed and should get financial support. County councillors in those days were almost always either staunchly Conservative or Independent, often local businessmen or shopkeepers, and by their nature not given to favouring the idea of subsidies, regarded as a socialist way of dodging the hard facts of life. All too often, their only contact with us had been to oppose our applications for fares increases in the traffic courts, very understandable from their viewpoint, but no help to us.

This was to be another area where good public relations work was to prove essential. A 20-minute presentation using countless slides and a commentary spoken by a professional broadcaster was prepared by Tony West's company at his suggestion, aimed at county councillors and emphasising the effect on elderly people and those without access to a car of service cuts. It was shown all over our area, and I am convinced that it, more than anything else, was responsible for increasing the amount of grant from the counties to the company in this period of a need for new understanding of the problems by hundreds of thousands of pounds.

Naturally, they wanted value for their money, but the avoidance of the very severe contraction of rural services that would otherwise have been inevitable played its part in helping to save the company as a whole, because it helped to spread the costs of providing garaging and maintenance facilities. We did have to close three or four garages in the more urban areas, where in some cases the pattern of services had made some redundant, the more viable services they ran going to other garages nearby. We did run into some trouble temporarily as a result of this because the engineering staff and facilities at the remaining garages couldn't cope for a time, but that was overcome by the much larger-scale reappraisal I have already mentioned.

Yet another problem arose towards the end of my spell with Midland Red. As part of a move to modernise the fleet, we placed an order for 100 lightweight Ford buses. At the time, demand for new buses was high and obtaining delivery in a reasonable time encouraged a turn to fresh suppliers, added to which the fact that the model was much cheaper than heavy-duty models was something we could not afford to ignore when the company's overall financial position was still very tight.

The model was the R192, which was popular at the time as a basis for coach bodywork among independent operators. They had 45-seat bus bodywork built by Plaxton to an outline not unlike that of the BET Federation design supplied to several BET companies, including that on some of our Leyland Leopard buses. The R192 was a front-engined model having much in

The 100 Ford R192 buses placed in service by Midland Red in 1970-71 seemed a good proposition at the time they were ordered, but proved inadequate for the type of duties they had to undertake. Rather as with the Albion Aberdonians we had run at PMT, the brake systems gave trouble when driven fairly hard and making frequent stops. On the other hand, an injection of a large number of smart new buses at modest cost had been welcome when there were problems in retaining enough maintenance staff to keep the fleet in good order. The Plaxton bus body had the same type of curved glass windscreen as had been standardised by BET for the Federation designs from 1963. No. 6355 is seen in Coventry in March 1971.

The Leyland Leopard continued to be favoured as a heavier-duty model, and a small batch of thirteen delivered soon after I left the company, in 1972, had Marshall 53-seat bus bodywork to BET Federation style - NBC tended to continue with existing standard types from both BET and Tilling sources in its early years. No.6465 was photographed in Burton in July of that year. These were the last Leopards with bus bodywork for the fleet however, as deliveries of Leyland National models began a few months later.

common with the Ford Thames Trader goods models of the time, but with the chassis laid out so as to allow the entrance door to be ahead of the front axle and thus directly to the left of the driver in the manner usual on modern buses.

The reaction to them was at first quite favourable. Drivers liked the light controls and car-like switches, and the noise level within was not as bad as some other models with the engine covered by a cowl within the body interior. They might have been reasonably successful if they had been kept to the quieter routes on which the heavier-duty models seemed to have more than enough durability than was needed for the job in hand, but this did not happen, partly because of the way in which duties were interworked, coupled to a general shortage of serviceable vehicles for reasons I have explained. There was a fuel consumption gain, with about 12.5mpg compared to about 2mpg less with Leopards or BMMO single-deckers on similar duty, and again this was welcome as a means of cost saving.

But then the problems began, at first in fairly minor ways but then becoming more serious, with the air-hydraulic brake system particularly requiring frequent attention to keep it up to scratch – there were clear indications that the compressor was barely on top of the job in stopping bus service, tending to run hot and then become carboned up. Most operators of the model rarely experienced comparable operating conditions and hence Ford which, as a large concern, tended to think long-term, being unused to making changes save on the basis of a future programme. It was rather like PMT's Albion Aberdonians all over again. Even in the country areas, buses were worked quite intensively to keep costs down, and virtually all duties included spells of hard work which revealed the shortcomings. The lesson was that the apparent savings of lightweight buses were often

illusory, and it is interesting that exactly the same conclusion was reached in detailed studies of whole-life costing made by NBC a few years later.

By the time 1972 came round, I had been with Midland Red for over five years. They certainly hadn't been easy, and yet Operation Phoenix had pulled the company round. The threat from West Midlands PTE was still there – Derek Fytche and I had fought hard to get a deal on the basis of an operating agreement, as was being hammered out both on Merseyside and Tyneside, where the NBC companies were set to continue to provide an important share of the services. On the other hand, dear old North Western had been destroyed in a deal with SELNEC PTE in the Manchester area, which transferred so much of that company's bus operations to the PTE that the rump was split between Crosville and Trent. It was ironic, quite apart from being sad for people like me who had associations with it from our younger days, for it had been efficiently run and among the most profitable in the group, and was an ominous portent of the threat still over Midland Red.

As it turned out, the matter was not resolved until after I was called to take a new job at NBC headquarters, but eventually in December 1973, what we feared did happen and Midland Red lost 170 services, 1,396 employees, 413 vehicles and six garages to the PTE, which took over all our operations which ran wholly within their boundary. No doubt from their viewpoint it made sense but it took the heart out of the company, in almost literal as well as metaphorical terms, leading to its break-up. I cannot help wondering what might have happened if we had been able keep it all together, for even today, I find that former employees still look back wistfully to 'the friendly Midland Red' of old.

Chapter Twelve: At 'The Kremlin'

'The Kremlin' was the usual nickname for the National Bus Company's London headquarters among senior management of the operating companies. This, of course, was in the days when the real Kremlin was the nerve centre of the Communist empire, controlling not only the Soviet Union but also almost the whole of eastern Europe plus many more countries and organisations in other parts of the world. Of course, NBC was nothing like that, but it was controlled from the centre to a degree more than many commercial groups and certainly more than BET's bus-operating business had been.

This was inevitable to some degree, since it was under direct Government control and, regardless of which party was in power, the Treasury influence was there, as I had been made uncomfortably aware during the Operation Phoenix exercise described in the last chapter.

When the call came in 1972 for me to become a member of the headquarters staff, I could not help thinking how strange it was that I, who had been at the forefront of the battle to keep BET bus companies out of Government control on two occasions almost a generation apart, should find myself being asked, just a few years after the second of these very public 'anti-nationalisation' efforts, to play a part in the running of the very kind of set-up we had sought so hard to resist.

Yet it would be unfair to portray NBC as some kind of ivory tower created on purely 'political' lines, for in many ways it was much more like the result of a normal merger between the BET and Tilling bus groups. At least the politicians had recognised that the only sensible way to run the business was to put people who knew the practicalities in charge, even if they were inevitably now under overall policy control from Whitehall. Even the use of the name 'Company' was a clue to a deliberate intention to run the set-up on lines which retained some elements from what had gone before – indeed, this had come as rather a surprise to some people, notably in the trade unions, who expected a re-creation of the British Transport Commission with its more civil-service-like organisation.

Almost all the senior staff were drawn from one or the other of the Tilling or BET bus empires, and the period between the announcement of the purchase of BET's bus interests by the then Transport Holding Company in November 1967 and 1st January 1969, when NBC came to life and took over the THC's bus operations in England and Wales, had been spent in setting up an organisation which in many ways was a cross between BET and Tilling. Such matters as the use of four-weekly as opposed to monthly accounting periods

had to be thrashed out so as to have one uniform system throughout the group. This sort of thing may seem simple, but the effects stretched through the whole organisation to all the local offices within the operating companies, so it was important to get it right, and as our experience at Midland Red was to show in the succeeding year or two, it was essential that we knew what was happening, especially in financial terms, right down the line.

Of course, as BET continued in being as a large group of companies, even though no longer operating buses in Britain, it retained its headquarters at Stratton House, in Piccadilly. The headquarters used by the Tilling companies under the Transport Holding Company were too small for the combined set-up, and hence a new home for NBC's head office had to be found. Tall office blocks were going up all over London, and it was one of these that was to be NBC's headquarters during the major part of its existence. The address was 25 New Street Square, but in fact the building occupied the centre of the square implied by the name, which was unusually small and situated in an area not far from Fleet Street which at that time was something of a mixture of the newspaper industry and the law, in terms of the type of business being pursued in most of the surrounding buildings.

Anyone seeing the eight-story building for the first time might well have thought it had the look of the proverbial ivory tower. Yet in fact, it was not all that large, the construction being such that the ground floor contained little more than a modest reception area and by the time I got there only about half of the building above was occupied by NBC – indeed we were short of space, as I was soon to find. I recall that a publishing firm, Benn Brothers, with which Tony Benn, the far-left Labour politician, was associated occupied the upper floors, and he could sometimes be seen going to and fro, although that was in no way related to our activities. By the time I arrived in 1972 the Conservatives were back in power following Edward Heath's success at the 1970 General Election, and Benn, though a former Minister, was on the opposition benches as simply a Labour MP.

My move to headquarters had an odd feel to it in another sense. For about five years I had been General Manager of the largest bus company in the country, although that job was far from being the proverbial piece of cake, as I hope I have conveyed in the last couple of chapters, and I was far from being a free agent, being responsible to my Chairman and through him to BET and subsequently THC and NBC headquarters in London. Even so, I was in charge of a big organisation, with a decent-sized office and such perks as a chauffeur-driven car – the latter not quite so much of a luxury as it may sound, bearing in mind the size of the company's area geographically and the need to be free to study relevant papers as I travelled about.

But in London, though it was a step up in overall rank, as NBC's Director of Property, I was now a relatively small fish in a large pool, or at least one with some very big fish in it. In practical terms, I now had a tiny corner waiting room for an office and had to share a secretary, and no longer had my chauffeur-driven personal car, which I confess was what I missed most. This was partly because no-one knew how my position would develop – I was the first incumbent of a newly-created post called Director of Property – within a few months it was renamed Director of Property Development, and the truth was that no-one knew how it would go.

The position of property in relation to the bus business was changing. In earlier times, it was probably true to say that not much thought had been given to the value of the property bus companies had in their possession beyond its function as garaging for the vehicles or, in some cases, the provision of bus station facilities for the travelling public. When first set up, quite often in the case of ex-BET companies going back to tramway days in the early years of the century, generally the land values had been low and the constructional costs had long since been absorbed. Yet in more recent times, particularly from the 'sixties, the value of urban property, especially in or near city or town centres, had grown enormously.

This had been made more evident by two factors – the need to assess the property values accurately in drawing up valuations for the purchase of the ex-BET bus assets by THC, and conversely by the way in which surplus garages were put up for sale as the services they ran contracted and were transferred elsewhere, as had happened with us at Midland Red. There had also been the need to assess the values of the Midland Red property when negotiations began over the proposal to transfer the set-up within the West Midlands area to the PTE – although we had still been fighting this when I left, we had needed to assess values in order to negotiate effectively. Indeed, the experience I had been forced by circumstances to build up in this field, coupled with more general managerial experience, no doubt influenced the decision to appoint me to this new post.

Another factor all too often apt to be forgotten is that the duties of the chief engineer of a bus company include responsibility for the care of the property as well as the vehicles. In a large concern, he would have a buildings department having staff of appropriate skills, possibly including an architect as well as foremen and workpeople used to dealing with building repair work to handle it, but he had to take responsibility and hence understand what was involved in order to make the appropriate decisions. So my days with PMT and, before that, in the engineering departments of other companies had given me useful experience.

Yet when I arrived at headquarters, I knew very little about property management, let alone development, as a field of policy. It was a new world, but in my favour was the fact that very few people with a background in transport did. What was more, the whole picture was changing. Rebuilding of urban centres was nothing new in itself, as the story of any big city reveals, having occurred repeatedly over the centuries, but from about the 'sixties, it had far more to do with the fast-rising value of urban land as well as of the buildings and businesses that could be put on it. Looking back, it seems clear that the need for obtaining expertise in this area and relating it to the practicalities of running bus services was largely my function.

It was certainly a voyage of discovery. I did have solid support from NBC's senior staff in this field, now brought under my control. At the beginning, H. A. F. ('Mick') Spooner was Co-ordinating Architect for Property Development, becoming Chief Architect. He had come from Southdown, where he had built up valuable experience in an area where land and property values had begun to rise before most other parts of the country.

However, a key figure was Aubrey Orchard-Lisle, who was senior partner of Healey & Baker, whose name is familiar to many thousands of home-owners as estate agents but whose status as property consultants gave them nation-wide status. The importance of his knowledge was recognised by his appointment on a part-time basis to the main NBC board from 1972 to 1976, coinciding with my period of involvement with this side of the business. He and I worked together a great deal over that period, and I would like to pay tribute to him – sadly, he died when this book was in its early stages. He was one of the world's perfect gentlemen, for, bearing in mind that I knew virtually nothing while he was a true expert, he never once said "This is how it should be done", treating me as an absolute equal.

Aubrey took me around property developments all over the country, and gradually I learnt to look at a depot in quite a new way, and instead of diving in to the detail of how it was operating by looking at the drivers' defect sheets, standing back and considering whether it could be used in some other way, enlarged or perhaps part of it turned into a series of shops.

Some of the decisions to be made were obvious enough. Quite often, there were numbers of terraced houses adjoining garages that had been purchased as part of the original deal, or sometimes with a view to possible expansion and retained so as to retain control over the possibilities. They often produced very little rent under the controls then in force and when it was clear they were not needed, it made more sense to sell them, often quite profitably. Other sites could be let and revenue obtained for them, all helping the company's overall finances even if not on a big scale at that stage.

This process was carried further in later years. There was a subsidiary called Omnibus Stations Ltd, formed way back in 1928, oddly enough to set up Lower Mosley Street bus station in Manchester, familiar to me since my boyhood, as a joint enterprise between operating companies, and this was retitled Omnibus Estates Ltd, to manage the property side of the business on a nation-wide basis for NBC. It acquired non-operational property from the subsidiary companies but its main function was to investigate the development potential of all the bus company sites around the country – as can be imagined, this was a huge task.

Omnibus Estates Ltd was managed by Fred Robinson, who had run Victoria Coach Station and when he became due for retirement, George Newman, who had succeeded him at Victoria, stepped into his shoes at my invitation in 1956. George has described how a system was set up in conjunction with Healey & Baker which provided for one of that firm's partners for a particular area to be made responsible for inspecting bus premises and reporting on the development potential.

It is important to recall that at that stage there was no thought of dismantling NBC. Even though it would not have been formed under a Conservative Government, the Heath administration of 1970-74 did not consider it a practical proposition to reverse what had been done, and was primarily interested in making sure it was run on sound business lines. When Labour got back into office in 1974, naturally its nationalised status was not questioned but, equally, the aim to make sure that costs were kept firmly under control was not in doubt – indeed, when there was a national financial crisis in 1976, the pressures on us to pay our way were very strong.

The immense amount of information amassed on property development potential took time to build up, and it is ironic to recall that the eventual beneficiaries of all the effort we put in were the purchasers of the NBC operating companies when they were put on the market a decade or more later. Some of my former colleagues who took part in management buy-out ventures are now millionaires as a result of the property potential included in the purchase deals they were offered very cheaply. In those and other cases the buyers were able to sell off bus station sites in valuable city centre locations and recover much of what they paid for the business as a whole.

However, as time went on, my activities took a different turn. In 1974, my title was changed again to Director of Property and Engineering. I felt particularly proud of this latter role, bearing in mind my ambitions going right back to childhood to be a bus company engineer. The board level structure of NBC had not

'The Kremlin'. The first headquarters building of the National Bus Company did indeed look like the proverbial ivory tower, but by the time I arrived on the scene as Director of Property, NBC occupied only the lower four floors – effectively three, since the ground floor was little more than a reception area, and I had only a tiny office. In fact, although decision-making was more centralised than with BET, the nation-wide organisation, in charge of a combined fleet of 21,000 buses and coaches in the earlier days, was run with far less head-office bureaucracy than might have been thought and, even at the highest levels, salaries bore no comparison to the figures that hit the headlines among privatised utilities today.

The value of property, especially in urban areas, grew enormously in the 'sixties and 'seventies, and the implications of this were to occupy a good deal of my time at NBC headquarters. Victoria Coach Station had been built in the 'thirties as a terminal for the long-distance services of various operating companies in the BET and Tilling combines. It thus became the focal point of NBC's express services running into the capital, which latterly adopted the name National Express, as seen on the white-painted Leyland Leopard coaches visible, and still a familiar sight today as the only fragment of NBC to retain the 'double N' corporate symbol. In this photograph, building work on the premises is evident – this added an extra floor, and NBC's headquarters moved from New Street Square, although that was not until 1982, after my retirement.

previously had a director with engineering specifically mentioned in his title, but there was and continued to be a Director of Technical Services then in the person of George McKay, most of whose career had been spent in various engineering posts within the Tilling group, culminating in that of Chief Engineer, though his speech immediately revealed his Scottish origins. He handled such matters as the relationship with Leyland, being on the board of Leyland National, as well as Bristol and Eastern Coachworks, all of which were jointly owned by Leyland and NBC. He was also NBC's representative on other bodies of an engineering nature.

Assisting him was Ken Batten, who had been appointed Administrative Officer, Technical Services in 1972.

Peter Wyke Smith, who joined the NBC headquarters team in 1974 as Group Executive – Engineering, had a similar career to mine, with an engineering slant, though in fact he had begun life intending to be a doctor. At one time, he had been with Midland Red, though before my days with that concern, based at Dudley garage, then progressing through company management with various concerns, latterly as Director and General Manager with Crosville Motor Services Ltd.

Also brought to New Street Square that year from Midland Red was D. V. Clarke, as Project Manager, Maintenance Costing, a subject in which his work was to provide a far more detailed view of what it costs to run a bus throughout its life than had ever been attempted before, showing incidentally that the lightweight bus was not as good a proposition as might be thought from superficial reckoning based on first cost, fuel etc. Over its whole life, maintenance costs rise to more than nullify the apparent savings. This was something which did not surprise me, with the experience I had with the Albion Aberdonians at PMT and the Ford R192 buses at Midland Red, but it led NBC to turn away from lightweight types such as the Bristol LH, on a basis of clear figures in terms of money which could be saved. The whole question of the costing of all aspects of bus operation was one in which NBC did outstanding work, and I would recommend today's budding bus managers to study some of the findings. In general, the foregoing were more concerned with the vehicle side than I was at this stage in my career, but one of the strengths of the concentration of talent at New Street Square was the breadth of experience from our different careers we each bought, and naturally exchanges of view fed into the policy we adopted.

I was particularly concerned with the choice of the most effective plant and equipment for maintaining the vehicles. Bus washers had to be both foolproof and designed to cope with the driver who was in a hurry, for example. The checking and, if needed, topping-up of engine lubricating oil levels was no longer a driver's job, as it had been in much earlier times, and devices such as the Frankmann system for automatic topping-up were of value both in saving a time-consuming and none-too interesting yet responsible job for garage staff and reducing the risk of engine damage due to human failure. Similar remarks apply to coolant level warning devices, though with both of these the reliability of the automatic system must itself be a potential source of trouble.

However, from 1977, there was another change of direction when my duties were revised yet again to become Director of Management Services, Consultancy and Property. I was sorry to leave engineering, though I remained in touch with my colleagues there in my new capacity. By that time George McKay had retired in 1975 and been succeeded as Director of Technical Services by Peter Wyke Smith and from 1977 his role was expanded to become Director of Engineering and Technical Services.

'Management Services' was a form of words to convey the aim of helping the companies to be more efficient, partly based on the experience, in which my story was far from unique at New Street Square, of rising through successive levels of management in operating companies. One of the things that was apparent when we had got to the top of the hill, as it were, was that the promotion prospects of potential managers from the engineering side in particular were hampered by the lack of adequate understanding of what was going on in the company as a whole. It is always a danger in any line of business where part of the job is getting one's head down and getting on with, say, making sure the buses are fit for service that the broader aims and problems seem remote.

Another area where help could be given was in taking advantage of the possibilities of computers, then still at a fairly early stage in their use as a business aid, and in which some of the larger companies, including Midland Red, had been pioneers.

Consultancy was a growing field of activity. It was becoming recognised that NBC had immense depth of knowledge. It was the largest comparable bus-operating organisation in the world, with 19,000 vehicles, down slightly from its peak in the early days, but still an immense concentration of expertise, large enough to enable many things to be studied by people with the best specialist knowledge available. There was a valuable source of income to be obtained in offering to help people in other countries develop bus operations.

The list of countries I visited, some of them several times, reads like a travel agent's brochure.

Nearest home, and the first consultancy exercise, carried out with David Deacon and Harry Tennant of Ribble, was the Isle of Man, then considering setting up what amounted to a smallscale version of NBC, a pattern that was to be found in quite a number of other cases. Then, in Europe, there were trips to France, Belgium, Spain and Austria. In once-familiar ground to me in North Africa, there were visits to Algeria, Egypt and Saudi Arabia. In Asia, we went to Pakistan, India, Sri Lanka and Singapore, and travelling further in broadly that direction, Australia.

In the Americas, working more or less from North to South; there were trips to Canada, the United States, Costa Rica, Trinidad, Barbados, Venezuala, Colombia, Brazil and Peru. The United States visit, to New York was of particular significance, as we were involved in discussions on United Nations aid programmes to improve transport services in under-developed countries.

It would be wrong to think that these were holidays, for there was often difficult and sometimes tricky negotiations where care has to be taken to avoid giving the wrong impression, but inevitably what tends to linger in the mind are the impressions gained in off-duty moments. We were often very kindly treated and the beneficiaries of people with great wealth, yet witnessed evidence of appalling poverty, sometimes almost in the same place. This particularly applied in India, where it had been arranged through a colleague that I would be staying with former High Commissioners in considerable luxury, with numerous servants and all possible amenities, yet barely round the corner there were people living in a shanty-town of cardboard boxes with no sanitation.

There was a certain amount of leg-pulling, particularly in English-speaking countries, such as in Australia, where I was invited to address a meeting of transport people in Melbourne, and I was tipped off that they would expect me to arrive wearing a bowler hat and carrying a rolled umbrella. I started off by explaining that "Even in the seven years I've spent in London, I've never worn a bowler nor carried a brolly, and with that out of the way, I'll answer any questions you'd like to fire at me." In fact, it went quite well, but it illustrates the misconceptions people have.

In other parts of the world, it wasn't so simple, with inevitable language problems for a start. Yet I have always managed to communicate by one means or another, gesticulating, use of eyes etc. Sometimes my extrovert ways would alarm my colleagues. For example, when visiting Saudi Arabia, where we had been asked to go after earlier consultations with the Board of Trade and London Transport had fallen through, one is warned in a booklet issued by the Foreign Office to be careful not to praise one's host's possessions because the Arab code of hospitality puts him into being obliged to give them to you.

So of course, we arrive by air and are shown into a marvellous Mercedes-Benz air-conditioned limousine for the journey from the airport to Sheik Omar's palace. It went like a dream and, of course, the first thing I said was "What a lovely car." Oh, crikey, what had I said! That happened about three times, but Sheik Omar later said "We know all about that booklet, and I can tell you this – we give what we want to give", which was rather nice. In fact I got on with him very well, and we were able to advise on the setting up of a local bus system on NBC lines. At the end was even able to make a joke about the verbal similarity between his name and mine, asking whether he thought I came from his antecedents or him from mine!

In other parts of the world, it could be more tricky, and sometimes in ways which had unexpected traps for the unwary. In Venezuela, we visted Maracaibo, which is an important centre in the oil industry. There is a huge market there but there was no decent public transport system beyond a sort of taxi service which operated very erratically. Peasants come in from all the surrounding areas, and even from across the border of Colombia about 100 miles away, to buy or sell produce – we were told there were over a hundred different kinds of beans, for example. We were studying the travel pattern with the idea that the location would make a marvellous bus station to act as a centre for routes coming in from the districts around.

We had been looking around for about 3 hours in a 100° F temperature and were dehydrated. I asked if there was anywhere we could get a beer. Nothing was visible, but eventually we located one and we settled down at the bar. After a while, a local chap came by on his way to the loo, wearing the most marvellous sombrero and of course I remarked on it, overcoming the language problem by tapping it to convey how impressed I was, repeating the process as he came by again. Perhaps fortunately for me, one of the locals came up and said that touching another man in Maracaibo was taken as a signal of homosexuality, and that a certain part of your anatomy was liable to be chopped off! Needless to say, my colleagues said "For God's sake Walter, keep your hands down."

However, I mustn't give the wrong impression about those last years with NBC. There were relaxing moments, and I was lucky enough to have the chance to see quite a few parts of the world on the consultancy side, but there was a great deal of serious work. In addition to the various fairly specialised duties I have described, as a member of the management committee of NBC chaired by the Chief Executive, I found myself having to participate in corporate decisions and hence to take a broad view on a wide range of subjects.

We were fortunate in having a remarkable range of talent, something that was dispersed when the decision was taken to split NBC up into small pieces when it was privatised, and compounded by the decision to throw away the route licensing system that had worked well for half a century in favour of deregulation, but I will go into that more deeply in the final chapter.

S. J. B. (Jim) Skyrme was Chief Executive during my earlier years at New Street Square, followed by Robert Brook from 1977, though additionally he became Deputy Chairman from 1978 and of course Chairman in later years, though that was after I had retired. Both, like me, had come to NBC from BET, with careers in the management of operating companies, and similar remarks applied to others with ex-Tilling histories.

Another duty I took on in my later years at New Street Square was acting as NBC's representative on the board of British Transport Advertising. Its Managing Director was John Nunneley, who had come to that post after a few years with British Rail – indeed that title (as opposed to the earlier form, British Railways) and the marketing name Inter-City were two of many innovations for which he had been responsible. He brought a new dynamism to transport advertising, and greatly increased much-needed revenue by ventures, sometimes controversial, such as the overall advertising applied to some buses (though they were limited in numbers, there being never more than 90 within NBC), and the T-shaped offside display on double-deckers. It was a huge challenge, and I found John Nunneley a remarkable man – I was happy to continue as consultant to BTA for three years after my retirement.

NOW I KNOW WHAT YOU MEAN BY 'IF'

VARIOUS 'IF' VISITS TO SAUDI AND OTHER ARAB COUNTRIES.

No, dear reader, my overseas consultancy trips really weren't like this, even though my colleagues and I were often very kindly treated. This cartoon perhaps conveys how those whose duties kept them at New Street Square thought I was occupying my time!

Chapter Thirteen: Some wrong turnings

It so happened that my retirement from direct active participation in the bus operating industry in 1979 almost coincided with a profound change of direction for both bus operators and manufacturers. I have been a life-long Conservative, and many of the ideas as expounded by Mrs Margaret Thatcher at the beginning of her term of office appealed to me.

In retrospect, the defeat of the alarming excesses of trade union power, which seemed to have got out of control, was a remarkable achievement – though I still have a great deal of respect for the old type of trade unionist, with many of whom I worked over the years – each side would argue its case with no quarter, yet there was a common sense of regard for the good of the industry and the public.

I, in my turn, had fought nationalisation with the whole of my being, both in the 1947-50 period and again in 1966-67 – indeed, though I could not say so publicly at the time, it was without doubt the biggest tragedy of my life when I heard at Midland Red that we, along with the rest of BET's bus interests, had been sold to the State. I have seen how the dead hand of Treasury control could inhibit enterprising management when I was helping to run NBC as a nationalised enterprise. Looking back, quite honestly, I feel that it was well run, thanks to the management inheritance it was given by BET and Tilling, and was perhaps the most efficient of all the nationalised industries. Yet if we had been able to apply BET's methods and commercial approach, I think it might have been substantially better. And by the way, I do not say that in any sense of disparaging Tilling, for the companies in that group were also run very efficiently, both before and after they became State-owned.

The idea of management buy-outs as a means of restoring the operating companies to normal commercial life made good sense, though I think the dice were loaded against the purchasers by the insistence on breaking NBC up into small sections with no cohesion whatever. It is interesting to see how something akin to the old groupings seems to be emerging with the growth of Stagecoach, Badgerline and others.

Yet when I look at the bus industry today, after nine years of deregulation, it seems a sorry sight in many ways. For a start, just consider the collection of buses one sees, all too often long overdue for replacement, certainly under the rules we used to apply within BET – for its policy, if applied today, would mean that anything older than 1983 would be either on its way to the scrap yard, or at least due for early sale. Next time you go out, just have a look at how many buses you see with registration numbers having suffix date letters

rather than the prefix-letter series introduced in 1983. If companies were able to apply a 12-year life, there should be no Bristol VRT, Leyland Atlantean, Leopard or Fleetline models in their fleets, and only a very few Leyland Nationals of the final type, for example. It is noteworthy, and I am sure it is not just coincidence that the bigger of the new groups seem to do a bit better in this respect, though in most cases there is still a long way to go.

We didn't run more than a handful of minibuses in the whole country in BET days, but feel sure that if we had, they would have been pensioned off considerably sooner than full-sized buses, say at a six-year life, which would mean that anything older than a F-prefix would be out, and that would knock out the big fleets of minibuses placed in service in 1986-7 that are still to be seen in many places.

In any case, I simply cannot see the minibus surviving as the preferred choice, save in very specialised circumstances. NBC bought them on a big scale right at the end of its existence as a means of coping with unregulated competition – in effect, it was almost a return to the ideas I recall from my childhood when, in the similarly 'deregulated' days of the 'twenties, operators sometimes ran a few nimble small buses – in some fleets they were called 'chasers' – whose function was simply to harass other concerns' buses working on the same route. The trend over the years, as the bus industry developed, was always to try to carry more passengers with fewer staff, so buses gradually got bigger and crews smaller.

The typical bus North Western used to run in the 'thirties seated 31 (in very comfortable seats, I might add) but needed both a driver and a conductor. Then, a little later, we ran a higher proportion of double-deckers, and single-deckers themselves got bigger after 1950. One-man operation at first was permitted only on little buses seating 20 or so, in many ways equivalent to today's minibuses, and generally only those companies with sparsely-populated territory, such as Crosville and Lincolnshire, ran them in any quantity – none of the concerns in which I served ran more than a handful. From the 'fifties it began to be applied to larger single-deckers, where we were able to carry up to 45 passengers without a conductor by about 1960, though quite a battle with the trade unions was needed to get it. Then it was the double-decker's turn, and we'd got to 70 seats or so with a crew of one by the time NBC was in existence. Crew costs have always been the main item to be covered by revenue from fares or any other source, and the minibus makes a nonsense of the need to keep that under

NBC went in for minibuses in quite a big way as one of its last moves before being broken up. The original reasoning, completely reversing the thinking of the previous 50 years and more, was to use them as a defence against unregulated competition. The initial exercise was carried out in Exeter by Devon General Ltd, a company title that revived an old name, using Ford Transit 16-seat minibuses. It seems ironic that in many cases, including the leading vehicle in this scene, the very simple conversion work from the van form in which they were supplied by Ford was carried out by Carlyle Works where, in earlier times, Midland Red had built its own, often very advanced, designs of vehicle. It came as no surprise that this early spartan form of minibus generally soon gave way to larger types.

control, even if its driver is paid less than his or her colleague at the wheel of a bigger bus. It is significant that many of the so-called midibuses now widely favoured are actually larger than the full-sized single-deckers of the pre-1950 period, which seems to suggest we are now treading the same path to a larger average vehicle size – in other words, sanity is prevailing!

Obviously, it is important to run a sufficiently frequent service to attract passengers where the traffic allows, but running hordes of minibuses where bigger buses would be more economic, perhaps as a means of competing with an existing service, seems to me to be a sure step along the road to bankruptcy. Indeed from what I've heard, minibus wars have left quite a few companies so strapped for cash that fleet replacement, already overdue, had to be deferred.

Another move which reversed earlier policy was the division of the larger operating companies. In Midland Red's case, the initial step in this direction had been the sale of the services within the West Midlands county area to West Midlands PTE, against which I had fought, but which came about in 1973. No doubt the division of the outer ring that Midland Red had thus become into four smaller companies seemed a logical step. Midland Red (South) Limited took over services in the Warwickshire and Oxfordshire area in September 1981, just over ten years after the Stratford Blue company had been absorbed into Midland Red, as conveyed by an illustration on page 67.

This scene in Stratford dates from July 1986, when the process of privatisation and deregulation was in hand. The Leyland Olympian bound for Birmingham was one of the last to the standardised design with Eastern Coach Works body to be supplied to NBC companies - the four Midland Red successor companies, like the rest of NBC, were soon to be sold off, in 1986-7. The ECW plant closed in 1987 and Leyland Bus, after struggling to survive as a management buy-out and then as a subsidiary of Volvo, eventually succumbed in 1993 – not unconnected events!

Even minibuses occupy road space, and indeed a couple of 16-seaters parked quite closely need nearly as much room as the 52-seat Leyland National seen struggling to find enough room to pull into the kerb; the latter also had the merit of needing only one driver. This scene in Dover, with car parking adding to the chaos, dates from early deregulation days, in April 1987.

It is possible to keep older fleets in good order, and indeed Tilling used a longer vehicle-life policy than we did at BET, yet its fleets were well maintained. But both BET and Tilling, as well as the Scottish Bus Group and all the major city fleets, ran efficient central workshops which overhauled buses and coaches to high standards. Such establishments are out of fashion today, and it is true that the better-designed of modern body structures do not need the frequent attention that applied when timber framing was common, though corrosion is still a problem with some well-known modern types. Some mechanical and electrical units can be handled on the basis of letting the manufacturers' service organisation handle them on a unit exchange basis via local dealers, though I wonder if the quality of overhaul is as good as we used to achieve.

There is another factor to be born in mind in the general condition of a bus fleet. That is that a regular supply of buses properly overhauled to high standards and not just given a quick coat of paint, added to an adequate supply of new vehicles, combine to keep up a good average standard for the fleet as a whole. This makes the garage staff's job of covering every duty with a serviceable and presentable bus one they can be expected to achieve. Neglect the engineering element of any organisation running vehicles and you are courting disaster, as was made clearly evident to me during my army days. We might well have lost a major battle in Italy when 70 tanks boiled up by the roadside when a minor modification had not been carried out, even though that episode was the proverbial ill-wind so far as I was concerned, for my appointment to put it right led to promotion.

In my days as a bus fleet Chief Engineer or General Manager, I used to go straight to the defect sheets on visiting a garage because I knew that was where I would find out if the garage staff were on top of the job. If work wasn't being done promptly, not only were unsatisfactory buses going out on service and liable to give a bad impression to passengers, but the drivers were liable to lose interest, fail to notify defects and so minor trouble could lead to a major failure and possibly even cause potentially dangerous faults to be overlooked.

I believe that there must be some degree of regulation to allow the operator who invests in new buses and looks after older ones to a high standard to have reasonable assurance that he will be allowed to recover that outlay from the fares of passengers. If a free-for-all is allowed, there is always the risk that another operator might decide to put a fleet of minibuses or cheap second-hand vehicles on a competing service and promptly cut off a substantial part of the revenue that could reasonably be earned.

In this sense, bus operation is quite unlike almost any other line of business. As soon as a bus has left a stop with some seats empty, potential revenue has been lost. A shop selling even the most perishable goods does have a further chance to sell its wares if the first potential customer decides not to buy. In practice, a bus operator knows that there will be some empty seats even on the most profitable kind of service, for example if travelling out of town on an early morning journey when the passengers are all going in the opposite direction. But if the 'good' journey is ruined from a revenue point of view by a competing bus, even a sensible calculation is thrown haywire.

In practice, there are many routes where the demand is enough to support a bus service running at a reasonable frequency, and a good Traffic Manager often will be able to judge the potential in advance – very often it will be already in existence. Allow someone else to muscle in – and if that firm is aiming to gain the traffic, that will tend to imply the provision of another similar service, quite often matching bus for bus. The end result is that both competitors become impoverished and even the winner of such a battle may be severely damaged, while the loser may well be bankrupt, especially if a small firm with limited resources. The vehicles may be sold off and find new owners, again by no means strong financially. So an increasingly dubious collection of used buses passes from operator to operator, steadily lowering the quality of service. The trail of business failures is not only wasteful, but passengers become bemused by the constantly changing routes and operators, adding to the tendency for those who have a car to use it or to travel by some other means.

Even the firm which manages to survive such battles is often in a poor financial state, unable to carry out the fleet replacement that was possible, and usual, in the half-century that the route licensing system set up by the Road Traffic Act 1930 was in force. It was introduced to put some sense into the chaotic era that had arisen the 'twenties, when an earlier era of 'deregulation' (though it was not called that then) had created problems not unlike those of today. To go back to that approach has been like going back to the dark ages in many respects, with 'fly-by-night' operators that arrive on the scene, doing great damage to the long-term provider of local services, and then either collapse into bankruptcy, or move on to create more damage elsewhere. The 1930 Act had its faults, perhaps sometimes discouraging genuine enterprise and certainly bus operators were often unfairly hamstrung by the degree of objection, amounting quite often to a complete veto, permitted under the system to the railways, but at least there was a degree of security of tenure. The Traffic Commissioners could, and did, work on a basis that major companies were expected to provide a comprehensive service in their areas, cross-subsidising the weaker routes from the strong. However, what was called abstraction of traffic, in other words allowing another operator to run in direct competition with the current licence-holder for a particular route was simply not allowed, for the specific reason that it was seen as weakening the financial position of the established operating concern and hence its ability to provide a viable network of services, some of which, in themselves, did not pay.

Inevitably, there was another side to the coin, in that Traffic Commissioners had to protect the public from the possibility of unscrupulous operators setting fares that took advantage of their monopoly position. As anyone who was involved in those days will recall, in practice, the boot was all too often on the other foot, for when costs began to rise on a regular basis as inflation began to get out of control, the operator had to seek permission for every fares increase, and that meant providing full details of the increases in costs. The process used to be so slow that we often hardly got the go-ahead for one rise before we had to put in another application, though the procedure was changed to minimise delay to some degree.

Certainly such a system meant that quite a lot of staff time was taken up with route licensing, fares applications etc. But at least we knew where we stood, and that if we ran the buses there wouldn't be someone else muscling in on the 'good' routes and thereby wrecking what were usually quite accurate predictions of revenue on which we could plan ahead.

Reliability of operation had been the watchword of BET, going right back to tramway days, and I still think it is essential for public transport to succeed in attracting passengers that buses run as time-tabled and that the routes and services should not be changed every few weeks. People need to know that the bus will run, rain or shine, and still be there to take them to work or to shop in a year's time, if they are to be encouraged to rely on it in their daily lives.

The importance of assurance of continuity and dependability as factors in building a lasting as well as profitable business was well understood by the founders of BET when building its network of electric tramways nearly a century ago. The proof of the soundness of their

Deregulation has had the effect of producing streets full of buses in some areas where operators think there is money to be made, but in practice many of the vehicles are almost empty. This simply means they are losing money, a situation which can only lead to the collapse of weaker operators and severe financial losses for the 'winners', discouraging investment in much-needed new buses. The scene shown was photographed in Piccadilly Gardens, Manchester, a city where about 70 operators struggle to survive and there has been a succession of bankruptcies, new operators – often short-lived – and takeovers which leave many passengers bewildered by the frequent changes.

thinking, followed in its basic philosophy by people of my father's generation as well as my own, lay in the survival and growth of nearly all the businesses they set up, converted to or expanded by motor bus operation, until the formation of NBC about 70 years later.

The provision of good public transport is, by its nature, a long-term business, something which seems to have been completely forgotten by some politicians with no background of knowledge in this field who thought they knew better than those whose livelihood and good fortune depended on getting the decisions right. One of the problems of our system of government is that a Minister, of whatever persuasion, is appointed to a field in which he or she probably has no experience and rarely is allowed to stay long enough to begin to understand its nature in any depth.

The 85 years of combined transport experience of my father and myself make some factors very clear, and if I may say so, some should surely have been obvious to people who claim to support the free-enterprise tradition. If the Conservative Party cannot see the needs of business out in the country as opposed to the city of London, it is in for a very thin time.

By its nature, public transport is a labour-intensive industry – there must be at least one person on every bus or train, properly backed up by those who maintain it, quite apart from those in the vehicle and other manufacturing industries which are key figures in the whole picture, and to which I will refer later in this review. It follows that keeping costs under control has always been of the essence, and the logical course is for efficient vehicles that allow as many passengers as practicable to be carried under the care of one driver to be used. Items such as fuel economy need to be watched, too, and even in this sense, larger vehicles are much more efficient.

I see three major worries:-

1. **Where does the capital come from, especially in the smaller businesses, to renew what are all too often old and 'tired' vehicles?** Quite understandably, the banks and finance houses are nervous when there is no security of tenure on the passengers' fares that provide the revenue.

2. **Where is the management training to come from in the future?** Here again, BET was running a good training scheme in my young days and I owe a great deal to it, but where is its like today?

3. **Where is the two-way loyalty that used to apply between operators, particularly their management, and the vehicle, bodywork or equipment manufacturer, with all its mutual benefits?**

This last, at least in part, has become a problem because of the poor overall financial state in which unregulated competition has left the industry.

It follows that, if operators can't afford new buses, their makers are bound to have a thin time. It is a great sadness to me, like many others, that factories, which not only built virtually all of Britain's buses but exported thousands every year, often no longer exist at all. Not that all the blame could be laid on recent events, for I feel it was a big mistake for Leyland to have allowed itself to be linked to an ailing and strike-prone car industry, back in the 'sixties. That led to starvation of investment capital away from bus manufacture, diverted into the bottomless pit of keeping the car business afloat, particularly when it was riddled with the effects of trade unionism of an extreme politically motivated kind. Yet the panic measures were insufficient even then to prevent what amounted to bankruptcy and hence involuntary nationalisation, with all the evils I outlined above in regard to the bus industry itself. Had the commercial vehicle business remained independent, the profits it would have been able to amass would have gone into keeping British firms in the forefront of bus design on a world basis.

As things are, we now have no more than a tiny part of what existed when I retired, even if the damage had begun earlier. AEC, Bristol, Daimler and even Leyland itself are all names of the past so far as bus manufacture is concerned, even if a modest part of Leyland's business lives on under the Volvo name, and using Volvo engines and other items in the Olympian bus designed, largely on the basis of liaison with NBC, by Leyland. Dennis still exists as an independent maker, and all credit to them for remaining flexible enough to respond effectively in a changing world, but for Britain to have only one bus chassis maker that it can call its own is an appalling result of a series of wrong decisions. And the idea of us running thousands of German-made minibuses, basically sound vehicles though they may be, does rather get under my skin.

Much the same applies to bodywork, for who would have thought, back in the 'seventies, that MCW (despite a venture into making complete buses, very successful for a while), Eastern Coach Works and Park Royal, quite apart from Leyland's own involvement in making complete buses at Workington, would all have gone? It is good that there are still some firms, such as Alexander, Northern Counties and Plaxton, who still build bus or coach bodywork in fair numbers and show how the nation's fleet could be renewed if only the circumstances were suitable.

But I have great faith in the ability of the British spirit to rise even in great adversity. Inevitably, at this time of the 50th anniversary of the VE and VJ days and the events of 1945, I cannot help thinking how we triumphed after the days of 1940-41 when we were all but alone against the strongest army anyone had ever seen. Even now, given the adoption of more sensible policies, there are enough people who remember how an efficient bus system could be run to get it together again. They, and maybe even more so the political decision-makers, could do worse than look back a bit to see if some of the lessons learned in the past might still be valid. I hope this book could set even a few people thinking, which is really why I set about getting the story of my father's and then my involvement down on paper.

APPENDIX I
The battle of Hammam-Lif, 8th/9th May 1943

An account of the exploits of 3 Troop, B Squadron, 2nd Lothians, whose Sherman tanks we had specially waterproofed, written by Lt-Col A. K. Waterston, at the time a lieutenant and leader of the troop.

During the final battle in Tunisia, B Squadron of the 2nd Lothians was under the command of Major "Bill" Anstruther-Gray, M.P., who had been posted to 1st Army to gain armoured experience before joining the Guards Armoured Division for the assault on the European mainland.

Because of his relative inexperience, the two senior troop leaders, of whom I was one, led the advance of the Squadron all the way from the breakthrough at Medjez-el-Bab to the outskirts of Hammam Lif where the Squadron found itself sitting nose to tail on the main road in a long queue of assault vehicles, after a very rapid advance against sporadic enemy action.

We had set off early after a rather sketchy breakfast and, as we sat on the road with crews on top of the tanks, the French locals came out with bottles of wine. As we began our second mug, at about "high noon", as the Americans would say, the celebrations were rudely interrupted by the arrival of six Nebelwerfer mortar shells in close proximity – our first introduction to the "Chicago piano"!

Consternation was complete but before dropping back inside the tanks and starting up, 3 Troop, to a man, knocked back their pints of vin rouge to empty the mugs and avoid waste. On an empty stomach, this made navigation somewhat erratic as we took to the fields, leaving the wheeled vehicles to their own devices. We progressed by putting our tank tracks astride a small ditch and proceeding in line ahead like a convoy of tramcars.

As our heads cleared, the troop took up position behind a hedge which gave cover from view from Hammam-Lif but after a time we were fired on from the flank by an anti-tank gun on the ridge to our right above the town. Fortunately, although reported as a 75mm gun it proved to be only a 50mm, which we were able to deal with, but not before troop leader singed his fingers collecting a souvenir armour-piercing round which he had watched all the way from the gun to the ground just beside his tank. Thus one learnt one of the lessons of war: solid shot on arrival tends to be rather warm!

That evening "Johnnie" Johnstone and I, the two senior troop leaders, picked our moment and suggested to the Squadron Leader that as we had been first over every ridge for five days and that even the most inexperienced troop leaders could hardly lose their way through Hammam-Lif we might be reserve troops on the

Sherman tanks of B Squadron of the 2nd Lothians with crews relaxing on VI (Victory in Italy) day, May 1945, on the south bank of the River Po. The more dramatic events involving B Squadron described in this Appendix occurred two years earlier in Tunisia when we were all rather too busy to have chance to take photographs. My duties had moved me away from the 2nd Lothians at the end of the North African campaign, but I remain proud to have been associated with them. The Shermans in the top row of this picture had 17pdr guns.

morrow. He agreed, but asked 3 Troop to establish an overnight road block on a 'Y' junction where the La Mahenmedia road joined the Tunis road just to the east of the town.

Having experienced a road block during the advance from Pickon to Kairouan, when a German half-track drove unscathed right through the middle of the 16 Squadron tanks, we set about our task with some care. Using damaged power cable which was lying about, we strung wires across all the roads at about head height and festooned them with blankets and tarpaulins. The idea was to cause any approaching vehicle to slow down enough for us to identify it and if necessary destroy it; firing by the light of the moon which was very bright. After a somewhat sleepless night on the alert with all guns loaded we were disappointed not to have put our tactical theories to a practical test.

In the morning, we had a good breakfast and stood by to await developments whilst the 10th R.B. and 'C' Squadron, with the help of the gunners, put in another attack. During this period, I walked towards the town in search of information and discovered an 'O' group of very senior officers indeed discussing what 1st Army should do next. (The regimental history of the event, published by the Lothians and Border Regimental Association reveals that they comprised Lieut-General Anderson, commanding the 1st Army, Lieut-General Horrocks – who was to become well-known later with his vivid TV accounts of famous battles – Major General Knightley, who commanded the division, and our own Brigadier, "Pip" Roberts.) I arrived more or less at the same time as a good "stonking" from our Nebelwerfer friend of the previous day, and was treated to the wonderful spectacle of the "Big Sunrays" taking hasty avoiding action.

Shortly after this, 'B' Squadron was ordered to move over the railway track towards the beach and 3 Troop moved off somewhat in the rear of the others although the enemy had begun to react strongly and we found ourselves in a certain amount of unpleasantness. I had little time to worry about this as in crossing the railway I got about four strands of telegraph wire round my neck which were steadily throttling me and preventing me from telling my driver to reverse. Fortunately I was wearing gloves for some reason and with the strength of desperation I managed to push the wires over my head before being catapulted out of the tank.

As this diversion subsided, it became apparent the Squadron had got a bit stuck and I was asked to find my way along a dry wadi towards the sea. This I was able to do and as the troop turned to run along the beach in line ahead things really got exciting. We were fired on heavily by a number of 88mm guns in a long clump of scrubby wood across the crescent of the bay. All we could do was speed up and move into the sea to try and get some hull-down cover. As the enemy shells hit the sea all round us, it was like a naval action with spouts of white spray rising 20 feet into the air. Indeed the only thing I heard on the W/T that I recall was someone reporting that they were being shelled by an enemy submarine. I must admit that in the very flat shore line the 88mm gun position was very like the silhouette of a submarine with guns flashing as they fired.

At this point I realised that I was the front tank of the front troop of the front squadron of the whole 1st Army and, what was more, there was no sign of any other tank behind me. I made urgent representations over the W/T to my two other tanks and after a short pause Sgt Ashen reported that Sgt Heston's tank had hit a mine. (It was only afterwards that I leaned that the driver, "Freddie" Barwell had been killed and the others wounded and severely shaken up.)

Sgt Ashen caught up and we turned sharp right off the beach into the town. I remember running over the trail of an antitank gun to make sure it could not be used again but I saw no sign of the gun crew. We then turned left down a tree-lined avenue with a lot of cattle wandering about or lying injured. The avenue was not wide enough for any tactical advance so we kept going flat-out with one tank each side until we came to a narrow part with a tight left turn back to the sea shore again.

I could not get round in one and I remember clearly having to jam the right sprocket of the Sherman into a house doorway, flattening the door into the front hall, to be greeted by the sight of about a dozen Arabs of both sexes stacked up the staircase, yelling and in a state of considerable alarm.

We got back to the beach and found things a bit quieter so moved on steadily to the far end of the town where we took up positions behind the last few outbuildings and hoped we would not be called upon to cross the open ground in front. It was a relief to hear that the Lancers were to pass through us and keep up the momentum. A few minutes later we saw a Lancer tank come along the beach and for some reason swerve into the sea and go straight on until it was swamped and the crew had to wade ashore.

I then became aware of a large concrete bunker about 150 yards to my front with a gun slit directly facing me. I fired an armour-piercing round from the 75mm gun which went straight through the slit and a figure appeared immediately, running towards me. This turned out to be a very brave gendarme who told me that over a hundred citizens had taken shelter in the bunker and please not to fire again. The situation could have been a disaster as my usual trap drill was to keep a high-explosive round "up the spout" and if that had been the case the scenes of carnage amid the confines of the bunker would have been horrendous.

For some time the only shell bursts near us had been of fairly large calibre, possibly from our own guns who may not have known that we had got so far. However these now ceased and I made contact with Squadron headquarters as they had now appeared just behind us.

The final episode before the supporting regiments moved through and left us to reorganise was the arrival on my troop front of a very shaken and rather fat German. He was the first enemy soldier that I had seen all day, alive or dead.

On his way to be interrogated by the Squadron

Leader, who was a majestic somewhat Churchillian figure, he had the temerity to light a large cigar to calm his shattered nerves. He might as well have lit a fuse under the officer in command of 'B' Squadron, who turned bright red with rage, seized the cigar and hurled it away whilst ordering our quivering Hun to stand to attention when addressing an officer!

Notes:
(a) From Gordon Goodrich's official account of this action, written as adjutant, it would appear that we were ordered to turn into the town off the beach. I have no recollection of this order but thought that I turned back into the houses because things were altogether too hot on the beach. However, if Squadron headquarters was anywhere close behind me I have no doubt that the order was given for the same pressing reasons.

(b) Peter Marey (2nd Lt.) only joined us two days before the Tunis thrust and I was asked to look after him until he found his feet. He was killed in the Hammam-Lif action through no fault of his own and it fell to me to deal with his mail. There was a letter from his father dated 10th May, asking what he was doing on the 9th, as his mother had woken him on the night of the 9th to say she was certain that he was in trouble as he had appeared to her clearly, sitting on the end of her bed, trying to talk to her.

(c) Immediate awards to 3 Troop 'B' Squadron.
240878 Lieut A. K. Waterston – Military Cross
7904781 Sgt Askew, H – Military Medal

Right: Some of those who served with the 2nd Lothians stayed in the Army in peacetime. Here Sgt D. K. Thomson, REME, formerly an A Squadron fitter with the 2nd Lothians is seen with a 1941 Leyland Retriever machinery truck which, although not intended for such duty, could tow a tank. Sgt Thomson transferred to REME and served as a civilian vehicle mechanic until disbandment.

Another useful vehicle was the Scammell Mark I tractor, nicknamed 'The Thing', seen here with AQMS W. Stoddart, REME, who joined a Light Aid Detachment working with the Lothians as a National Service craftsman, serving until disbandment.

APPENDIX II

Helen's Story

We met in a tent in North Africa on a hot July night in 1943. He was Captain James Walter Womar, R.E.M.E., age 25, 26th Armoured Brigade Field Workshops, and I was Nursing Officer Helen Hall Smith, age 24, Queen Alexandra's Imperial Military Nursing Service reserve – a Nursing Sister with 104 British General Hospital, El Arrouche, both serving with British North African Forces during the period of the 1939-45 war when the campaign in that part of the world was at a key stage.

Wally was seriously ill with M.T. Malaria, very weak, dusty, sweaty, in need of a shave and had just arrived on a Red Cross train from Tunis to Robertsville. I had been posted on night duty at lunchtime, having snatched a few hours sleep in the small tent I shared with another Sister. Anti-mosquito regulations caused me to wear half-sleeves attached to my grey and scarlet dress, men's battledress trousers underneath and greasy mosquito-repellent cream over wrists, face and neck. It was hardly a romantic beginning!

'K' Block had been newly erected to cope with the expected convoy of evacuated military personnel from Tunis. It comprised four large tents to hold 24 beds each and, in the centre, a small square office tent which accommodated medicines, syringes, drugs, sterile dressing drums, etc with a trestle table to write up reports on patients. Also there was the dreaded primus stove (which frequently blew out with gusts from the Sirocco) on which syringes and needles were sterilised, tea was brewed and special food for dangerously ill patients concocted.

A Royal Army Medical Corps (R.A.M.C.) orderly had arrived, saluted me briskly, and said "Private Bristow reporting, Sister". By lantern light, we gazed at one another in amazement – during the previous winter, as Staff Nurse on the Men's Surgical Ward at the Kent and Sussex Hospital, Tunbridge Wells, I had trained Pte. Bristow in hospital ward procedures. Now, we set to work with a will, to make up 96 beds with mattresses, pillows, sheets and mosquito nets. I had to indent to the stores for equipment, medicines, quinine, disinfectant, urinals, water, cutlery, tin plates, towels, soap and even a chair to sit on to write my report of the night's events.

I admitted Captain Womar, washed him and made him comfortable and somehow produced a tomato sandwich which was the only thing he fancied to eat. During the night the ward filled up and by the next night all 96 beds were occupied. More blocks of wards were in situ in preparation for anticipated casualties as the invasion of Sicily was about to commence, on 10th July.

But to begin at the beginning . . .

After the first world war, my father was offered an Army officer's family assisted passage to Canada. My mother's sister had married a Canadian artillery captain and her other sister had sailed to Canada on a two-year teaching exchange. So we settled near them in Ontario in 1924. I have very happy memories of swimming in Lake Ontario, streams and ponds during hot summers and skiing in the snowy winters.

My brother and I attended public school and high school, or Collegiate, as it was called, and when my parents decided to return to England in 1936, David and I were filled with dismay. I found myself beginning a new life and a nursing career as a lowly probationer nurse at Queen Mary's Hospital for Sick Children, Carshalton, Surrey, and three years later emerged as a Registered Sick Children's Nurse. I applied to the Kent and Sussex Hospital, Tunbridge Wells to undertake my general training, which I was allowed to complete in two years rather than three because of my R.S.C.N. certificate. As London was enduring fierce night bombing raids by the Luftwaffe, prospective nurses were asked to apply to provincial hospitals for training. Even so, there were air raids, as well as the wartime problems of the black-out and food rationing, but I passed my final examination in November 1942 and became a State Registered Nurse. I rushed out to buy my blue belt and silver buckle and wore bows under my chin with pride – I was a Staff Nurse!

At the end of February, after three months as a Staff Nurse, I decided I did not want to do mental nursing, fever nursing or train as a midwife; I wanted to join the Army like my father to be an army nurse in grey and scarlet. So I volunteered, was accepted, gave in my notice and with a first-class travel warrant arrived at Hatfield House, Hatfield, Herts (then in use as a military hospital) on April Fool's Day, 1943 as a new recruit in Q.A.I.M.N.S.R.

We were taught to salute, injected, had dental and medical checks, equipped with uniform, trunk, bed-roll, canvas bed, bath, basin and bucket. The contingent of 100 nursing sisters to complement the staff of the 104 British General Hospital sailed from Avonmouth in the hospital ship Newfoundland on 20th June. There were red crosses painted on the ship's sides and a large red cross on top was illuminated at night. We slept on the hospital tiered bunks which were provided to carry the wounded home on the ship's return journey. We were ordered to wear men's battledress trousers while at sea, in case the ship was torpedoed, U-boats being an ever-present menace. (Although hospital ships were supposed to be immune from enemy attack, there could be no assurance that this convention would be respected.

Indeed, it is sad to have to recall that the Newfoundland was bombed by enemy aircraft while off Salerno about three months later, suffering heavy casualties among the nurses, although I was at El Arrouche by then.)

After a brief stop at Gibraltar, it was portholes closed and an overnight dash to Algiers. We were billeted for one night in an infants' school and used our pristine bed rolls for the first time. Unfortunately the 'loos' were also infant-sized! Next we boarded the train travelling overnight through Algeria, eight to a compartment, dressed in our grey and scarlet worsted wool suits, lisle stockings, collar and tie and cap – the heat was well-nigh unbearable!

At noon next day, we were met at Robertsville station by some of our R.A.M.C. doctors and sergeants and driven in large lorries to El Arrouche, where our field hospital was being completed. 'Field' is right, for the hospital was sited in three or four harvested grain fields, a mass of tents of all shapes and sizes. The sisters' compound had rows of tents, two of us sharing each, the furnishings consisted of two camp beds with mosquito nets, two trunks and one canvas wash basin and bath, all on an earth floor. There was also a cookhouse and mess tent. Beyond, in another field, the R.A.M.C. doctors and surgeons had their own compound.

The hospital wards, kitchen, stores, operating theatre and admission post occupied further fields, along with R.A.M.C. orderlies and maintenance staff.

It was intensely hot and our food was corned beef in every guise, plain 'hard biscuits', margarine and dehydrated vegetables, with one mepacrine and one salt tablet daily. The mepacrine tablets made us feel queasy most of the time but Matron Owen said "You were not brought out here to catch malaria or be ill!"

But I must return to the events in 'K' Block. After a few nights, some patients were evacuated to the 103 British General Hospital, Captain Womar among them. I was not sorry, for as he began to get well he kept teasing me!

I nursed many soldiers from the 6th Armoured Division, Lothians, 17th/21st Lancers, as well as 8th Army veterans, many of whom had desert sores. After a month on night duty I had two nights off. Another sister and I decided to hitch-hike to Phillipeville on the coast for a swim in the Mediterranean – anything to get cool.

Miramar was a superbly beautiful bay with cliffs on both sides. We had a refreshing bathe and decided to eat our sandwiches. There were only about half-a-dozen people about and it was so peaceful. Then a tall man in a bathing suit walked over and said "I want to thank you, Sister", and I recognised Captain Womar. He offered us a lift back to the hospital in his utility, which we were glad to accept, as we had had an unpleasant lift there with a Frenchman who kept trying to paw my knees. As a 'thankyou', we invited Captain Womar to come to our compound dance and to bring a friend.

About this time, the Colonel had done an inspection of our compound with Matron and was astonished to find two bottles of whisky or gin underneath many of the

Here I am, back in wartime days with 'Captain Womar', as I first knew him, and his Austin utility, a welcome lift in which was indeed to prove a turning point for both of us.

sisters' camp beds. It is an old army custom that officers are issued with one bottle of spirits per month. A few older sisters, aged about 30-35, enjoyed a glass of whisky with a game of bridge but most of the younger ones did not drink, so what was to be done? I volunteered to ask Captain Womar if a bar, with pigeon holes for bottles, could be made in the R.E.M.E. workshops, This was done and we duly signed for our visitors' drinks and the rest put in a pool for the monthly dance. We were never short of partners!

The hospital was busy all summer but when I did get a half day off it was great fun to go swimming with Wally, and he made fabulous tea in a billy can. We sometimes exchanged cigarettes with the local Arabs for eggs which we would hard boil, or for a melon.

We became engaged on 9th September, and a small party was held in an olive grove by Wally's commanding officer, Major Desmond Gadsby, who highlighted the occasion in spite of meagre rations, equipment and cutlery.

The rainy season arrived, with mud everywhere. Colonel Scott issued us with men's battledress and boots. Glamour was forgotten as we huddled round our Beatrice stoves sipping cocoa at the end of an exhausting day on the wards. On night duty, our unwieldly boots and clomping footsteps on the wooden duckboards kept the wounded Tommies awake, though they never complained.

December brought a sad parting for Wally and me. He was posted to Algiers to Allied Forces headquarters, while I also found myself on the move. The 104 hospital was packed up, the patients were evacuated and we all embarked on the Hospital Ship Oxfordshire bound for Italy. What luxury – hot water, baths, showers, white napery, butter, fresh bread rolls and delicious food. Such a change from that eternal corned beef in its various guises. In this sense, those elegant naval nursing sister were to be envied, yet not one army nursing sister

Walter and I, on honeymoon during 48 hours leave, on the island of Ischia, a few miles from Naples in June 1944.

On 4th May Allied Forces headquarters was relocated at Caserta Palace, a few miles north of Afragola. Wally arrived at the 104 and found me, on night duty! It was wonderful to be together again after 5 months and we decided to marry as soon as the Army could process our papers. The great event took place on 1st June, 1944 at Christ Church, Naples, which is the Anglican church in the city, and our hospital chaplain, Captain Currie, officiated. The Q.A's had filled the church with flowers and dear Col. Elwes, R.E.M.E. gave me away. Capt. Harris, R.E.M.E. was best man and Nursing officers Joan Westwood and Charlotte Walker were bridesmaids, while many off-duty hospital staff and R.E.M.E. colleagues supported us in church and at a reception held in the Sisters' Mess at Afragola. Matron Vera Owen allowed me 48 hours leave for a honeymoon and the navy sailed us to the Isle of Ischia in the Bay of Naples.

When I reported back on duty, I learned that Rome had been declared an open city, 'Jerry' had retreated and the 104 was soon to move up to Rome where a proper hospital had been allotted to us. We took over the Italian Military Hospital, which had recently been under German control, near the Colleseum. Meanwhile, Wally was promoted to Major, and commanded his own workshops near Forli on the east coast of Italy.

We next met at Christmas, when he had seven days leave and came to Rome. Matron could not spare me as the hospital was very busy indeed, with full wards of casualties from the battles over the mountains and up the coast to Rimini and Ravenna. I was allowed two sleeping out passes and the usual off-duty time, afternoon or evening. So I organised several of my Q.A. chums to go to the Y.W.C.A. to have lunch, tea or dinner with Wally if I was on duty. One day at the end of the week, the receptionist at the Y.W.C.A. said to me "I am sorry indeed to have to tell you this, Sister, but your husband has had a different Q.A. for lunch, tea or dinner nearly every day!" "I know," I replied, "I sent them."

During the freezing winter of 1944-5, I worked on a surgical ward; admissions, operations, amputations, transfers and evacuations seemed endless. The troops were wonderful to nurse, so bodily fit that there were very rarely complications after surgery, and they were always uncomplaining and cheerful.

Wally had moved up to Rimini with his unit and at the end of February received a signal from the R.T.O., Rome:- 'Lt. Womar arriving to see Major Womar'. I had two nights off after a spell of night duty, so accepted a lift in a Jeep from a Major returning to the front from leave in Rome. It was a long and hazardous journey, across the mountains, with perilous passes, mud and blown-up bridges. As I had been on duty all night, I kept falling asleep, and finally the major asked if he could tie me in as I lolled dangerously as we lurched round the hairpin bends. I was dropped off at a Y.W.C.A. hostel and spent a happy time with my beloved husband of six months.

I asked Matron Owen for a posting up forward, and in March found myself, trunk and bedroll on a Red

would have changed places, for all our hardships.

After Christmas in a transit camp feasting on Sorrento walnuts and carrying logs in for the hut stove, we were on duty once more. The 104 had acquired a convent building suitable for use as an operating theatre and surgical wards, the medical cases and convalescents being housed in huts and tents in the grounds. It was at Afragola, just outside Naples, which suffered frequent air raids in the port area because of the shipping activity in support of the Army as it fought its way northwards.

The hospital began admitting casualties evacuated from the casualty clearing stations during the fiercely-fought battle of Cassino and the Anzio beachhead. Soon the wards were full and there were patients on stretchers between beds. Everyone had to work hard and non-stop. Then, in March 1944, Vesuvius erupted. The volcano was about 6 miles away, and it sounded like a continuous thunderstorm; at night the sky was lit up scarlet and fiery red. Most of the patients were evacuated and we were left to sit on packed trunks and ponder our future! I remember being sent on leave with another Sister to the officers' leave hostel in Sorrento, which was the Hotel Excelsior Vittoria, where the patios, verandahs and walkways were 2in deep in lava ash. Nowadays, that hotel is the most expensive in the town.

Cross train bound for the 83rd B.G.H. at Cesena, near Ravenna. However, it was not long before that hospital, and Wally's R.E.M.E. workshop advanced north as our troops liberated Italian cities and crossed the River Po. Finally, the Germans surrendered to the 8th and 5th Armies in Italy on 3rd May. The hospital settled at Udine and began admitting casualties, and the R.E.M.E. workshops, after a spell at Rovigo, moved back to Riccione by the Adriatic.

After the war ended in Europe on 8th May 1945, married Sisters were repatriated first, and I sailed home in July from Naples on H.M. Troopship 'Batory' with some 4,000 on board. I slept on a mattress on the floor. It was a sad parting from Wally, but as the war was over, we were at long last able to think and plan for our future in peacetime Britain.

It was wonderful to be reunited with my father and mother again, for I had not seen them for two years, and also to meet my brother David, whom I had not seen since 1942. He was now a Flying Officer Navigator, with D.F.C., having completed two tours of duty in Lancaster bombers, latterly in the Pathfinder force which led the large-scale raids on Germany.

Life in Kent had not been easy, with the V1 flying bombs and V2 rockets even after the conventional air raids had ceased. I met my in-laws for the first time in London and both families got on famously – I was delighted to have a sister-in-law!

In August, I had a letter from Italy – Wally due home on 28 days leave, by train from Rimini via Milan and Calais. He arrived on 14th August at my home in Kent to meet his in-laws for the first time, and again all went well. Next day, we travelled from Euston to Stockport, where his parents were overjoyed to see him safely home after three years at war. But he had to return to Naples for nine more months until his release from the Army in May 1946. In the meantime, I learned to cook and to plant a garden, as well as shopping for some of the necessities for our future home.

Wearing a regulation navy chalk-striped suit and a trilby, Wally was demobbed and we had a brief holiday in the Lake District together with a somewhat embattled second-hand Vauxhall 10 car – like everything else, cars were scarce and expensive. It was decided that Wally would embark on a three-year management trainee scheme which his father had piloted for B.E.T., to commence on 1st July at Maidstone & District. We found some digs and set about working and living in peacetime England on £5 per week – less than a bus driver's pay. We were now the lowest of the low, very different from service life.

Food was rationed, 'on points' (another form of rationing for certain items) or unobtainable unless one queued. After six months in digs, we bought our first home, 90, London Road, Maidstone and moved in during the freeze of February 1947. Coal was rationed, central heating almost unheard-of, and we borrowed coupons from the family for curtain material. There was a garden, which we tilled assiduously, and we took a lodger (another trainee) for a guinea (£1.05) per week,

all found, and I returned to nursing in the Casualty Department at the West Kent Hospital, Maidstone, to help pay the mortgage – when Wally wasn't working, he was studying and, overall, life certainly wasn't easy.

In April 1949, we moved to Newcastle on Tyne, where Wally was appointed assistant to the General Manager of Northern General Transport Ltd, Major Hayter. To get a flat, at 102 St Georges Terrace, Jesmond, we had to tell a fib and say he was Assistant General Manager. This time there was no garden, but we secured an allotment on the Town Moor, setting forth with rake, hoe and spade to walk three blocks to tend our vegetables on most Saturdays.

As we both hoped for children and I did not become pregnant, we both underwent tests which proved inconclusive but not very hopeful. Therefore we decided to adopt a baby, filling in all the necessary forms and were put on a waiting list. I was lonely at the time, feeling rather strange in the North of England and missed the busy hospital life with built-in friendship and colleagues. However, on the whole, we enjoyed our time in the North East, especially on New Years Eve, in those days little observed in most parts of England, but there celebrated in much the same style as in Scotland. The friends we made there have been lifelong, in particular Bob and Peggy Bailey and also another trainee, Len Higgins and his wife Peggy.

After two years, Wally was again promoted, this time becoming Chief Engineer at Eddison Plant, based at its headquarters at Belton, near Grantham. We were extremely fortunate to be able to buy a house with a quarter of an acre of garden nearby, and felt like a King and Queen.

I wrote to the adoption agency in Newcastle on Tyne to tell them of our change of address, only to be told in reply that as we now lived in a different county, our application was cancelled and we must apply locally – this after a two-year wait. It was a sad setback for me, and I shed not a few tears. However, eighteen months later, we were overjoyed to adopt a beautiful little baby girl of five weeks – Jacqueline Joy – by that time I was 34 and Wally 35, and we were a happy family in our lovely home and garden.

A family at last. Walter and I with Jackie in October 1954, when living at Belton, near Grantham.

Friendships flourished – Leslie Suter, who lived two doors away with his wife Lily, had been a R.E.M.E. Major at the Palace of Caserta when I had first met him in May 1944 as a colleague of my future husband – it's a small world. We used to sleep the three sons of John Spriggs, the capable Manager of Eddison, every December while their parents attended the annual B.E.T. Dinner Dance at Claridge's in London, given by Harley Drayton, the group's Chairman. We had no inkling at that stage that one day we would be going to Claridge's!

Once again, Wally was promoted, this time to become Chief Engineer of a bus company – Potteries Motor Traction at Stoke-on-Trent. We moved in September 1958, our Grantham house unsold, and with no money to mortgage another. So we decided to have a modest house built and pay in instalments. Meanwhile we rented a house in the country, Field House, Onneley, Cheshire – very rural, with cows and fields and Jackie now aged five attended the village school a mile away, which necessitated Wellington boots and the climbing of stiles. It was a delight to find that Bob and Peggy Bailey lived within easy reach in Newcastle-under-Lyne, Bob being P.M.T.'s Traffic Manager. Over the years, our two families shared many Christmases, birthdays, picnics, etc.

Six months later, we moved into our new home, 40, Allerton Road, Trentham. It was compact, with a tiny garden, but we were happy to have our furniture out of storage and even found room for the dappled grey rocking horse, so kindly lent us for Jackie by Mr Collie of Kingston Depot, Eddison Plant. I rejoined the Women's Institute, learned to drive – eventually becoming the proud owner of a VW Beetle and volunteered for the W.R.V.S. to do 'Meals on Wheels'. I had to drive a temperamental Thames van with a hot box and Wally cautioned me not to have an accident with one of his buses in the winter fog. While at Trentham, we found that Potteries people were very friendly. We keep in touch with one very special family to this day and our meetings are as full of fun as in the 1960s.

Wally was promoted to become General Manager of P.M.T., a great surprise and pleasure, so much so that we quite forgot to eat our dinner that evening. So he had made it at last and the management training scheme had been worthwhile all those years earlier in 1946.

Yet, four years later, in 1966, the Womar family was again on the move – would we never settle? – for Walter was appointed Deputy General Manager of the Birmingham & Midland Motor Omnibus Co, to quote the then full name of what was far better known as Midland Red, and the indications were that he would succeed Donald Sinclair as General Manager, as indeed happened a year later.

As Jackie was an only child and our family had frequent moves, and transport wives were expected to attend the numerous company and civic functions, we thought it prudent to send her to boarding school where she would have a more settled eduction. So, from 1964, Jackie was educated at the School of St Mary and St

Jackie with Walter, about to set off back to boarding school at Abbots Bromley from our home near Kidderminster. Car enthusiasts will recognise the model as a Humber Super Snipe.

Anne, Abbots Bromley.

In 1967 we had a great shock. B.E.T. had 'sold out', for all its bus companies were to be nationalised – anathema to Walter, and indeed we had both been involved in the campaign against this back in the days with Northern General Transport and when the threat returned at just about the time he went to Midland Red he had been in the thick of the battle right up to receiving the news. Even so, life went on, now as part of the National Bus Company, and indeed Wally was appointed a Director of Midland Red in 1969.

We were living very happily in the country near Kidderminster. Then in 1972, the prospect of a move came yet again. Once again, Walter was promoted, this time to National Bus Company headquarters in London, where he was appointed an executive Director. Neither of us were keen to live in or near London, and after much heart-searching, we decided that I would stay on in our home, which was also not too far from Worcester, where Jackie was at teacher training college. Walter would commute, staying in London between Monday and Friday, with weekends at home.

This mode of life continued for eight years, and our marriage survived happily in spite – or maybe because – of it! But we shall always be grateful to Guy and Ruth Newbury who offered Walter accommodation in their town home. Guy was also an N.B.C. Director, in his case in charge of one of the regions, and their background was quite remarkably like ours, he having been a Major in the R.A.S.C. and then a B.E.T. trainee and his wife had been a Q.A.I.M.N.S.R – they had even been married in Italy.

Walter travelled abroad for National Bus and regaled me with tales about Venezuala and Saudi Arabia, to name but two, on his return. I should have loved to accompany him but of course we could not afford it, and a nationalised company could not do so either. I filled the weekdays with gardening, Red Cross – I supervised the Medical Loan scheme in the area – and helped with the Disabled Club as a driver, and was appointed to the Parish Church Council. We had many visitors to stay with us – family, friends from other countries we had lived in, and my brother and his Canadian wife Robyn and their two sons were at last able to visit us from Vancouver. After years of separation these were very happy occasions.

We are enjoying our retirement holidays in Italy, Malta, Amsterdam, Vancouver and Toronto. In 1984, we held our 40th wedding anniversary at home and were so fortunate that our bridesmaids were present for a jolly week-end – Mrs Stan Straub (Nursing Officer Charlotte Walker, Q.A.I.M.N.S.R.) and Mrs Joan Foster (Nursing Officer Joan Westwood, Q.A.I.M.N.S.R.). At the end of that year we sold Glovewood and moved to our present home at Low Habberley, Kidderminster, with its delightful garden.

Looking back, we have much to be thankful for. Although I was an indifferent starter I have since realised that I enjoyed my time as a busman's wife.

Walter and I returned in 1988 to Ischia, where we had had our brief honeymoon in 1944.

And on the same trip, we took this photograph of Hotel Excelsior Vittoria, Sorrento, where I had been sent on leave when Vesuvius erupted in March 1944. It was then an officers' leave hostel, and should have been quite glamorous even in those days, but the effect had been spoilt by a 2in layer of lava ash on the verandahs and walkways.

APPENDIX III

Engineering Management of Tomorrow

This is a shortened version of a report I wrote in October 1979, when Director of Management Services, Consultancy and Property of the National Bus Company. Many of the circumstances under which it was written are so different to those applying today as to make it seem as if from a different world. Some of these, such as the rapid turnover of staff, reflected the relative ease with which employees, especially if skilled craftsmen, could find other work, notably in manufacturing industry, at that time.

On the other hand I feel that the need for care in attracting recruits of the best quality at all levels, and to ensure that they are properly trained to enable the best of them to take up senior posts, is as valid as ever. I also believe that engineering still provides an excellent background for General Manager posts in terms of the breadth of understanding of bus operation, provided that Chief Engineers have sufficient chance to become familiar with the directly commercial side of the business. Clearly small organisations cannot provide much in the way of organised training for senior posts as provided by NBC or, before them, BET, but I feel sure that the large bus company groups now emerging will find the need for such provision if they have not already done so.

Introduction

A broad brush approach separates the engineering function into four areas, namely:-
(a) Chief Engineer, hopefully aspiring to General Management;
(b) Assistant Chief Engineer; Technical Assistant; Area Engineer;
(c) Those who have the ability, after training, to rise to a supervisory level – Chargehand, Foreman or Depot Engineer;
(d) Those who will always remain as manual workers either at depot or central workshops level.

The Chief Engineer of today

In assessing the present situation regarding promotion of Engineers to General Management level, we are faced with a real problem.

Because of the very nature of his duties, the Engineer does not become closely involved in the commercial management of the company during his day-to-day activities. The Traffic Manager and Company Secretary are more directly concerned with such activity and in consequence are, to a certain extent, automatically trained whilst carrying out their normal duties.

To compete in the General Management field, the Engineer has to apply himself diligently to functions outside his own discipline in order to measure up at interview, but more importantly, to fully understand the commercial and accounting sector. However, in view of the increasing pressures placed upon the Engineer, he does not have the time to occupy himself in any great depth with such matters.

However, given time and training, the professional engineer has the ability to direct his energies towards these wider objectives and in fact, having achieved them, will often emerge as a more comprehensively capable manager than his colleagues in the accounting and operating fields.

In the first instance, it is the General Manager's responsibility to see that this disadvantage the Chief Engineer suffers is corrected, particularly if he is based away from headquarters. We need to provide the necessary additional training for those with ability to develop their potential. We need, under Common Market conditions, to produce high-quality professional Engineering Managers with proven academic quality, which means being a Chartered Engineer and/or holding a university degree. I believe that a well-designed variation on the Senior Management Training Scheme will meet the requirements to equip such a person to run an Engineering Department and also satisfy his professional body.

The professional Engineering Manager of tomorrow

There is now a need for senior engineering staff, and therefore potential General Managers, to have university degrees. The objective is to enable NBC not only to build up a number of senior engineers with good academic backgrounds, but equally to train them in management and ensure that they satisfy the Chartered Engineer's qualifications through the Institution of Mechanical Engineers.

Engineering graduates, particularly those with manifest ability, can join a manufacturing organisation with the knowledge that hard work, application and successful results will lead to senior appointments. Such surety is needed in our industry, if we are to attract and employ the right kind of staff. Mr P. H. Wyke Smith's paper 'Engineering Objectives', as adopted by NBC, states that "Training programmes for a planned supply of qualified engineers lies at the heart of the Group's need to move forward on the objectives set down in the paper".

Universities are creaming off people we would

normally have employed years ago, but now that our salaries are more attractive we should take a fresh initiative and find out who is in charge of engineering at various universities. We should stimulate interest in the Chief Engineer's job and enhance it, sweeping away the impression that a bus company Engineer is little more than a glorified mechanic.

There should also be a more helpful approach to university students seeking to undertake project work, since the writing of a thesis will help to forge links with universities; so too would an invitation from NBC for graduates to undertake work of an investigative nature (e.g. the exercise at Trent Motor Traction into operating problems with epicyclic gearboxes).

Supervisory staff

One of the problems currently facing the Group is that key engineering posts, particularly at depot level, are in a number of cases held by staff not having the right inherent qualities. This situation is not of their making, but has arisen insidiously over the years as increasingly, applications and consequential appointments were adversely affected by remuneration levels and conditions of unemployment. It will take a long time for these responsible positions to be filled with the right quality staff.

Depot Superintendents have specialised and skilled staff under their control, and they require the skills to direct and apply such staff to the tasks within the depot. The Northern Regional Training Committee has identified six areas where training is immediately required to enhance the level of basic skills covering supervision. These are:- communication; industrial relations; work organisation; industrial legislation; motivation, and vehicle service training. The Group provides courses for engineering staff but unfortunately these are not usually followed up when they return to their companies. It is recommended that the initiative taken, in co-operation with Northern General, to produce a manpower training guide, be followed up.

Apprentices and craftsmen

There is a need to determine the potential of recruits from school and other places of work in order that their potential can be realised and used. It is essential to forecast the future requirements of apprentices, bearing in mind labour turnover, changing fleet sizes and more complicated vehicle types. A shortlist of apprentices should, at interview, be asked about their ambitions by the Chief Engineer and then seen at regular intervals as an encouragement towards realising their potential.

Labour recruitment, selection and retention

A recent report showed that 37% of all voluntary terminations took place during the first four weeks of employment and a further 17% during the following eight weeks. To help this 'induction crisis', it is important that the recruit should have a thorough understanding of the type of work (plus the ability to do it), the payment system (including bonus) and the working conditions at the time of engagement.

It is recommended that an analysis of turnover or absence be carried out regularly and maintained at head office or area level. The situation regarding shortage of spares has reached such proportions in the minds of employees as to have a detrimental effect on morale. Young unmarried employees tend to have the highest turnover rates as they have fewer financial commitments and are more mobile and ambitious. Other than personal or disciplinary reasons, the amount of money an employee could earn elsewhere is the primary reason for departure.

Conclusions

1. A more equitable balance is needed between the three disciplines, i.e. engineering, traffic and accountancy, at higher management level. Group strength is achieved by harnessing the skills and knowledge of the three prime functions on which the transport industry is based. Therefore, an attractive Senior Management Training Scheme is necessary for selected professional engineers, enabling them to be equipped with the skills of General Management.

2. We need to know our existing staff at all levels. Consequently, we must have manpower planning in-company, forming part of the Group scheme. This will provide an appreciation of training needs.

3. We should be closely associated with the labour market place, with close local contacts with universities, schools, technical colleges and Job Centres, etc for recruitment into Group and company training schemes.

4. Having ascertained our labour requirements and the sources of recruitment, we need to attract and retain the staff. We must have good publicity material of every nature, well-designed and comprehensive training schemes and a clearly recognisable management progression system.